Distressed or Deliberately Defiant?

Managing challenging student behaviour
due to trauma and disorganised attachment

Dr Judith A Howard

First published 2013
Australian Academic Press Group Pty. Ltd.
Level 5, Toowong Tower,
9 Sherwood Road,
Toowong QLD 4066, Australia
www.australianacademicpress.com.au

Copyright © 2013 Judith Howard

Copying for educational purposes

The *Australian Copyright Act 1968* (Cwlth) allows a maximum of one chapter or 10% of this book, whichever is the greater, to be reproduced and/or communicated by any educational institution for its educational purposes provided that the educational institution (or the body that administers it) has given a remuneration notice to Copyright Agency Limited (CAL) under the Act.

For details of the CAL licence for educational institutions contact:
Copyright Agency Limited, 19/157 Liverpool Street, Sydney, NSW 2000.
E-mail info@copyright.com.au

Production and communication for other purposes

Except as permitted under the Act, for example a fair dealing for the purposes of study, research, criticism or review, no part of this book may be reproduced, stored in a retrieval system, or transmitted in any form or by any means electronic, mechanical, photocopying, recording or otherwise without prior written permission of the copyright holder.

National Library of Australia Cataloguing-in-Publication entry:

Author:	Howard, Judith A., author.
Title:	Distressed or deliberately defiant? : managing student behaviour due to trauma and disorganised attachment / Dr Judith A Howard.
ISBN:	9781922117151 (paperback)
	9781922117168 (eBook)
Notes:	Includes bibliographical references
Subjects:	Dissociative disorders in children
	Attachment disorder in children
	Attachment behaviour in children

Dewey Number: 618.928588

Cover photography © Tahnee Webb
Cover design by Maria Biaggini — The Letter Tree
Typesetting by Australian Academic Press Group Pty. Ltd.

To Izack

You were the original inspiration for this book.

You taught me so much about seeing through the behaviours to the child beneath.

You inspired me to keep learning and keep helping. I promise you, I will.

Contents

INTRODUCTION — 1

CHAPTER ONE
   Managing behaviour in schools — 9
      What do we believe about managing these students' behaviour? 10
      How do these students present at school? 13
          Rodney 14
          Garry 15
          Taylor 16

CHAPTER TWO
   Attachment and trauma — 19
      Let's talk about Attachment 19
      Bowlby and Ainsworth: Two early theorists with important messages 24
      The neurological and physiological impact of disorganised attachment 30

CHAPTER THREE
   The science lesson — 31
      The nervous system 31
      The human brain 33
      Neurons and synaptic activity 36
      The early childhood brain 37

CHAPTER FOUR
   What does this look like at school? — 41
      Fight, flight or freeze! 41
      Revisiting Rodney, Garry and Taylor 43

CHAPTER FIVE
What can we do about this — that works? 47
Relationships (both the problem and the solution) 47
Emotional self-regulation 52
Six-element model for student support 53
A list of recommended strategies and approaches 58

CHAPTER SIX
Crisis management 69
Preparing for and managing a behaviour crisis 69
Example of a crisis management plan 72
Helping teachers to understand and manage their own reactions and emotions during and after crisis. 75
Considerations for school policy 77
Suspension and expulsion 77
Moving a student to a new school 84

CHAPTER SEVEN
Compliance, adolesence and working with parents 85
Recognise difficulties with compliance for what they are 85
Physiological and social concerns in adolescence 86
A note on working with parents 87
A final word… 90

BIBLIOGRAPHY 93

Introduction

He didn't sleep well. There were dreams, mostly bad dreams. They weren't so much scary, although they verged on it at times. Rather, the dreams were disturbing; just disturbing enough that it was important, very important to keep waking himself to stop them from continuing. There were times when he awoke that he could hear the screaming and the thuds but he was well practiced in pretending that they weren't real and insisting his body go back to sleep; at least until they stopped. His restless, young body had pulled the bed covers from where they had been firmly tucked that morning. The pillow was now lying on the floor; its cover now faintly but permanently stained with the remnants of his perspiration. He knew it was becoming lighter so he squeezed his eyes more tightly shut to resist the knowledge that another day was beginning. He pushed his arms out to search in vain for that pillow that he might be able to pull over his head to keep out the emerging sounds of voices and movement.

The woman's voice was dry and emotionless, telling the children to get up. The man's voice was raised and demanding that she keep the noise down and to shut the baby up. He knew that pretence of sickness or blatant refusal would get him nowhere. He had tried both many times before and rarely succeeded in avoiding getting up and facing the day. He really didn't want to leave her or leave the home but knew it was unlikely to be avoided.

His mother rarely spoke during breakfast, except to tell him and his sister to be quiet or to do as they were told. He wished she would smile more and maybe even let him sit on her lap sometimes. He didn't ask her for this though. He remembered her saying last week that she could tell that her new baby hated her by the way he cried and struggled when she fed him. He wondered if she thought that he hated her too and maybe that was why she never smiled.

His stomach felt uneasy most mornings; today it was in knots. He had memorised the script about breakfast; that it was the most important meal of the day and that he should be grateful that it was provided to him, considering the lot of others throughout the world. Besides, he was the oldest and should be a good example for his brother and sister. The morning news barked out reports of child pornography on the internet, earthquakes, floods and war in countries far away and grief, loss and terror closer to home. He succeeded in swallowing two small pieces of very slowly chewed pieces of toast. The rest he "wasted". He tried to avoid staring at the bluish tinge around her cheekbone but it seemed to be growing and darkening as he chewed and he really wanted to look at it.

He dressed slowly. Each piece of clothing, each shoe, each sock representing a further commitment to enter that zone he dreaded. He packed the lunch he knew he would never eat and the books in which he knew he would never write. He searched for her asthma puffer. Eventually he found it under her handbag, beside the lounge room cabinet. He squeezed it into her left hand before he trudged through the front door and slowly moved onwards towards the bus stop.

He was last to leave the bus, followed closely by the driver's raised voice telling him to go straight to the office to report his behaviour. Although he was only looking at the ground, he could feel the driver pacing behind him, the closeness just as real and just as uncomfortable as it would be if his big hands were clamped down on his shoulders. He paced to the rear door of the office, with head down, his shirt hanging out and his bag dragging along the concrete path.

He arrived. He shouted. He pushed. He swore. He cried. He attacked. He refused. He was removed. He was punished. He left.

Another day at school. He was 7 years old.

It is not unusual for teachers to be confronted with the annoyance of having to deal with challenging student behaviour. Despite our preference that it is not so, student behaviour does tend to have a considerable impact on the delivery of teaching and learning programs and, in many cases, the personal or emotional wellbeing of teachers, both during school and after hours. In most cases, teachers accept this as part of their professional experience. They speak of good and bad years and great and no-so-great classes that they have taught and, more often than not, these evaluations will refer to the types of student misbehaviour they have needed to manage. Details of these good and bad years and great and not-so-great classes tend to fade from memory over time.

However, teachers can find it very difficult to erase from their memories the particular type of student who will be discussed in this book. They tend to easily recall these students by name, even many years after they have moved on from their classrooms. They report uneasiness when working with these students and feelings that there was something "not quite right" with them. They remember how quickly and unexpectedly these students flew into behavioural outbursts with little warning and as a result of no clear triggers. They suggest they had much difficulty getting through to these students or just when they felt that they did, that the students would then sabotage the relationships in some way, leaving them feeling surprised and perhaps, shocked, hurt or annoyed. They recall these students having extreme challenges responding to adult authority and having even more trouble with relating appropriately to their peers. These students tended to respond poorly to tried-and-true behaviour management processes that worked well with the rest of their students. Often, the behaviours of these students left them with little choice but to resort to withdrawing them from class activities or removing them from class altogether. It is likely these students would have been suspended or perhaps even expelled from school at some stage. Dealing with the needs and behaviours of these students was a daily occurrence, leaving teachers feeling tired and dissatisfied with their jobs, and perhaps leading them to taking more days off work than usual. Indeed, teachers often reflect that the period of time they spent teaching these students was a time when they questioned their capabilities as educators and sometimes even their choice of career.

The writing of this book was driven by the outcry of a growing population of school educators and child and adolescent support professionals in health or child protection systems, who were feeling they were becoming less and less effective in addressing the complex needs and controlling the often dangerous and disturbing behaviours of these types of students. Similar to the young boy described earlier, students from troubled homes and histories were arriving at school with already elevated levels of stress hormones raging through their bloodstreams, racing heartbeats and distracted and confused thought patterns. Their nervous systems were firing erratically and their innate threat detectors were already on guard. With these students, trouble would more than likely commence on the bus ride to school, let alone after they walked through the front gate.

A further complication was becoming evident in the students' homes. Foster carers desperately needed schools to keep these students at school five days a week so that they could cope with the significant demands of caring for a complex child or adolescent. However, schools were often in the position of needing to send the students home due to extreme and challenging behaviour. All too often, this caused much friction between home, the various support agencies involved with supporting the students and the schools. Sometimes, as a result of this friction, foster placements failed and students were required to change schools to accommodate a new home placement, which, of course, led to them suffering further disrupted attachments.

So, this book has been written in a sincere attempt to address these concerns. From the school's perspective, dealing with the behaviours of one or more of these students within a class can seriously disrupt the day-to-day running of an education program, can present safety risks, can raise parent and community concerns and can impact on the emotional wellbeing of teachers and other staff members. New teachers question their decision to enter the profession and more experienced teachers question their capacity to continue. In such an important and valued (or sometimes, undervalued) field as the education of children and adolescents, it is vital that we do not lose any more of our skilled and dedicated educators to the stress of this type of behaviour management concern.

However, and most importantly, this book has been written to support one of the most vulnerable and needy groups of young people in our society. The students who will be discussed have experienced trauma, both inside and out. Some have lived through emotional, physical and/or sexual abuse or serious neglect. Some have been adopted after spending their early years in war-torn parts of the world or in under-resourced orphanages. Many are under child protection orders and are living in foster care or group accommodation programs. All have experienced, to a greater or lesser degree, disrupted, absent and/or harmful caregiving during (at least) the first few years of their lives. All are living with the neurological, physiological and behavioural outcomes of what is referred to as "disorganised attachment".

It is important that the reader understands that when this book refers to trauma, it is not referring to one-off traumatic incidents such as a car accident, earthquake or death of a loved one. Of course, it is acknowledged that these types of traumatic events can have a huge impact on a young person and can leave them suffering what is often referred to as "Type 1" or "Simple Trauma". However, this book is focusing specifically on "Type 2" or "Complex Trauma". This type of trauma is ongoing and persistent and includes that which is experienced through continued physical, emotional or sexual abuse or neglect. This is the type of trauma experienced when a power relationship is abused, allowing an older person to harm a vulnerable and powerless infant or young child.

- In the first chapter of the book, I encourage the reader to examine what we truly believe about student behaviour management and I introduce the idea of viewing things a little differently when we are considering the behaviours of this type of student.
- Chapter Two overviews some important concepts from attachment theory and trauma theory that are vital for educators to understand to be able to better address the behaviour concerns of these students.
- Chapter Three looks into what I refer to as "The Science Lesson". In this chapter, the reader is taken on a journey to understand the neurobiological dynamics that have a direct impact on the behaviours of these students at school and that also provide clear direction for what needs to do be done to address them.
- In Chapter Four, we examine what all this might look like in a school context. We explore why these students can defy rules and authority, why they can abuse even the most supportive of relationships and why they can continually put themselves at risk.
- However, we will not stop there as there is good news to share! Chapter Five provides information and ideas supported by neuroscience that can be used by schools to minimise challenging behaviour and to enhance the education and overall wellbeing of these students. The (now outdated) belief that we are neurologically "hardwired" is clearly debunked and evidence is provided to show that particular school practices can lead to the "rewiring" of young brains.

This is not a group that usually responds well to generalist behaviour management strategies and certainly not to harsh discipline. They tend not to respond to a "short-term fix" or a "trial and error" response. To see progress, we need patience and persistence and we need to ensure that our efforts are grounded in solid research that addresses the specific needs and circumstances of this particular student group.

- Chapter Six will focus on ways that schools can effectively manage behaviour crises and disciplinary responses such as suspension and expulsion.
- The final chapter provides some additional information on student compliance, particular issues that can become evident during adolescence and issues when working with parents.

I do ask (if I may) that you read each section in the order provided and (please) do not skip to the section on "strategies". Over the many years that I have spoken to educators on this topic, I have found that most are very keen to discover strategies they can use to help "fix" these kids or their behaviours. However, the best outcomes come from educators and schools who have grown in their knowledge of the "science" underlying the problem and the potential solutions and who have also examined their personal and group beliefs before they use the recommended practices in their planning and intervention processes.

May I outline a few early points for consideration prior to the reader continuing to read this book?

- Stories I have used throughout this book are composites that have been drawn from cases with whom I have personally been involved or have known. However, they do not represent any one student. Also, in order to protect the confidentiality and rights of students and their families, school personnel and other professionals, names and autobiographical details have been altered in every case described.

- To simplify the text, the male gender is mostly used during general discussion about children and youth and the female gender is mostly used to represent educational staff. There is no prejudice implied by this.
- While the text will often refer to "the teacher", the information in this book is equally important to and relevant for any school personnel working with students. It should also prove helpful for practitioners from government or community child and adolescent support agencies that collaborate in interagency case support of students.

Chapter One
Managing behaviour in schools

Student behaviour management has become a very real part of teachers' professional experience and there are ever-growing expectations for schools to further develop their educators' expertise within this field. Many amazing thinkers have provided us with a multitude of valuable theories and techniques to help prevent challenging student behaviour from occurring and to minimise or address such behaviour when it does occur. Some teachers new to, and established within, the profession joke about "never smiling during the first school term" in their efforts to establish early their control and required classroom behavioural standards. They clearly communicate their authority and their right to encourage and dissuade particular student behaviours through reward, punishment and other processes. In many cases, these teacher practices are drawn from whole-school frameworks, supported by policies that articulate what is approved student behaviour and what is not, and how the adults running the school will respond to each.

However, general behaviour management is not the topic of his book. Rather, this book will focus on the very specific needs of a particular student group that is causing growing concern within our schools. Despite this group being small in number when compared to overall student populations, it has proven to be disproportionately concerning and costly for schools. These students can require inordinate amounts of staff time and school resources to teach and manage and, despite the investment, concerning behaviours can persist.

What do we believe about managing these students' behaviours?

If we are going to work constructively with these students, it is vital that we first examine our own beliefs as educators. In schools, there tend to be some recurring common beliefs about this challenging group of students, namely:

- We cannot expect these young people to behave any differently with such poor role modelling from the adults in their homes.
- These young people are victims of what we have in the past referred to as the "Cycle of Abuse", where children are doomed to grow up to re-enact the abusive or neglectful types of parenting behaviours that they received.
- These students tend to have an overwhelming tendency to control others to get their own way.
- These students just do not care. They just have no empathy for others.

Unfortunately, all these beliefs do have elements of truth and later in this book we will look into some of the reasons why this might be so. However, an unfortunate outcome of holding on strongly to these types of beliefs is that some educators may place these students into the "too hard basket", giving up on their efforts to enhance the life experiences of these young people or to engage or re-engage them in their schooling.

There is a further belief that is very influential and quite common in our schools that can often seal the fate of these students. This is the belief is that these young people have the **power to choose** to do what is right or what is wrong and that they are deliberately doing the latter. This belief is readily reinforced by the range of behaviour management approaches or systems that emphasise the student's capacity for personal choice, that tend to work well with the majority of students. We believe these particular students are choosing to deliberately defy us when, with a bit of effort, they could choose an alternative path, modify their behaviours and become more compliant with our expectations.

This belief, that these students do have the power to choose their behaviours, is very often associated with three closely related beliefs that I like to refer to as **"rights beliefs"**.

- First, many educators strongly believe that the **rights of the majority of students should certainly override the rights of a small minority**. They understandably believe that it is unfair to contribute disproportionate amounts of material resources and teacher time to one or a few students. This is a very powerful belief that is ultimately strengthened when resources are limited and class numbers are high.

- Second, many believe that the **rights of the teacher to teach** should override the rights of these students. Educators rightfully believe that they have worked hard to become specialists in the delivery of curriculum and to enhance student access to learning and can feel offended when the behaviours of a small minority of students continually impinge on this perceived right.

- Third, many strongly believe that the **school has a right to uphold its reputation** in the community. They can feel that the presence of students with very challenging behaviours may deter families with more promising and compliant students from enrolling or maintaining the enrolment of their children. They worry about the public inference that they may not be effective disciplinarians or classroom or school managers. They are concerned about the impact of this type of community opinion on future support and resourcing for the school.

Now, if an educator or a team of educators hold on strongly to these **"rights beliefs"** and at the same time believe that these students with problematic histories have **the power to choose their behaviours,** then withdrawing them from class or suspending or expelling them makes a lot of sense. Interestingly, if it is decided to use these types of excluding responses to student behaviour, educators tend to often hold onto two further beliefs.

- The first is that this form of discipline will be **good for them.** They feel strongly that someone needs to take a strong stance with these young students and, by their doing so, the students will learn to choose more appropriate behaviours in the future.

- The second belief is that if these students are going to continue to deliberately defy authority, refuse offers for support and cause ongoing difficulties, they just **may not deserve** access to the schooling opportunities that are on offer.

In this context, with these types of beliefs, **intensive behaviour support** may not make much sense to schools. Why should they use supportive, alternative, resource-intensive processes when the behaviour choices are deemed to be deliberate, the students are not responding to established behaviour management processes and staff and other students are suffering as a result of their behaviours?

However, there is a growing body of research on early childhood trauma and disorganised attachment (that will be shared with you throughout this book) that has now thrown up huge challenges to these types of beliefs. While it is agreed that these students can be oppositional, defiant and resource-intensive, research is now clearly showing that with some of these young people with troubled life histories their power to choose their behaviours might be seriously prejudiced. It is telling us that these students may be suffering significant impairment in so many areas that make up what it is to be a social and learning human being. It is showing that excluding practices do not lead to improved behaviour and, if anything, can lead to more complex, dangerous and self-harming behaviours in adolescence and adulthood and a seriously impaired capacity for parenting. These students can be hard work, but unless we deal with their needs in a constructive way we tend to see damaged students being further damaged through a variety of school practices, growing up to damage themselves, others and their own children (our next generation of students).

Challenging our own beliefs and the beliefs of our colleagues in this area is no easy task. We are educated people who educate others and it is confronting to consider that our beliefs about our core business might be either incorrect or inappropriate. This is why it is vital that school personnel are given access to the latest information and research about the connection between disorganised attachment, trauma, child development and school behaviours. It is also vital that we understand that this is a growing area of research that is only recently reaching schools. We should not feel affronted or guilty that we may have been using less than adequate approaches to educating, managing or supporting these students. Rather, we should be reading, accessing training and developing our practice, just as we would normally do for other areas such as curriculum content and delivery. Hopefully, your reading this book is a step in the right direction for you!

How do these students present at school?

Let me introduce you to three young boys. To start, I will describe only how these students presented at school. I will describe the challenges faced by their schools as they dealt with (or tried to deal with) the quite concerning behaviours of these young students. Later in the book, we will revisit these three boys to view their school behaviours through what we have learned from neuroscience.

Rodney

Rodney arrived at his new school in Year 2 and within weeks, his teacher was at his wits' end! Rodney's behaviours had quite successfully disturbed not only the smooth running of his classroom, but had a significant impact on most of the school. Rodney had the face of an angel — fair hair and blue eyes. He was just a little smaller than his peers but he certainly fitted into the average height and weight range for his age. He presented (mostly) as sweet; almost sickly sweet. He smiled a lot — even at inappropriate times. He loved to chat to others but often did not make a lot of sense during extended conversations. It was very usual to see Rodney following teachers around the grounds during breaks, engaged in quite constant chatter. He certainly preferred the company of adults to that of his peers. He had much difficulty sitting still during class and would often rub up against adults or wrap his arms around them. He chatted incessantly during lessons and experienced serious learning difficulties.

Rodney was a compulsive (and incredibly skilled) thief. He stole anything: food, pencils, books, marbles, jewellery, money, bits of rubbish out of the bin, pieces of old wire — anything. It was extremely rare that anyone actually observed Rodney actually take anything, yet multiple times each day, objects would disappear. Rodney always denied that he stole anything. When accused, he would make quite intense eye contact with his accuser, take on the persona of one who was so desperately hurt by such a cruel accusation and, with tears in his eyes, plead for his innocence to be recognised and believed. Strangely, Rodney would exhibit slight muscle spasms during any such period of interrogation that were not evident at other times. His facial muscles might twitch every so often, his shoulders might jump or his arms or legs might jerk just slightly. The movements seemed automatic, and if you observed Rodney closely he seemed to be using all his efforts to control his body, as if it was betraying him by revealing his guilt. It was at times like these, or when stolen items were forcibly taken from Rodney, that you could sometimes see the seething anger and fear underlying that sweet face.

Rodney would hoard his stolen items and then bury them in secret spots around the school. He would dig them up at opportune moments, stuff them into his pockets, down his socks, shirt or underwear and take them home. The school organised a daily routine with Rodney's family whereby he would be frisked when arriving at home and any stolen goods returned to school by an older sibling. This routine was successful for a short time until Rodney learned to hide the goods before arriving home.

Staff and students were furious with him — no-one was safe from having something taken. They increasingly withdrew from any relationship with Rodney and he became more and more isolated. Many school routines needed to be altered. All classrooms (doors and windows) needed to be locked at any time they were not occupied. Extra staff needed to be engaged during breaks to monitor Rodney and more and more students (and their parents) were becoming extremely upset about having their possessions or lunches taken.

Garry

By his first year in secondary school, Garry had already been expelled from four different schools. When he was at school, he was often being disciplined for disrupting his class or for task refusal, bad language or physical aggression. Garry attended school irregularly and often did not spend much time in class when he was at school. When he did attend, it was not unusual for him to spend most of his day outside of the classroom as his teachers considered him to be a safety risk to both them and their students. Garry was often placed outside the principal's office to complete his school work.

Staff at his school described Garry as "dark" when he became angry. When school personnel confronted him or insisted he do something he did not wish to, he would avoid eye contact, often staring at the ground, and his face would literally become darker in tone. His muscles would tense and he would not speak, except for the occasional short and threatening use of bad language. Even those staff and students who wanted to help Garry, knew to keep their distance from him at these times.

The school was aware that Garry was regularly in trouble with the local police and had received charges for a number of offences, including breaking into local stores and theft. They had needed to collect him on numerous occasions as he wandered the streets during school hours, sometimes even wearing his school uniform. Police officers had been called to the school when Garry had become too aggressive for staff to manage. When this happened, he displayed minimal respect towards them; often yelling, arguing and swearing. On more than one occasion they needed to restrain Garry as he attempted to either attack them or to run off.

Garry was addicted to cigarette smoking and was sniffing paint on a regular basis. His diet and hygiene were poor and his teeth were decaying. His uniform was often dirty. He had serious learning difficulties, often truanted and mumbled when he spoke so that it was often quite difficult to understand him.

Taylor
Taylor enrolled at her new school in Year 5. She arrived with a powerful reputation for highly disruptive and disturbing school behaviours and she had attended many different schools. She rarely responded when spoken to but was often verbally disruptive during lessons. She would drag her desk to a corner of the classroom and try to barricade herself in by stacking objects around her. She would collect some of these items from her home or other environments outside of school. This stacking behaviour caused difficulties for her teachers and peers as it would create further congestion in already crowded classroom spaces. However, when attempts were made to remove these

things or to move Taylor's desk, she would become very angry and aggressive.

At times, Taylor would just "explode" behaviourally. If she was in the classroom, she would throw objects, smash windows, knock over furniture and purposefully and forcefully empty out the contents of her classmates' desks onto the floor. If she was in the playground, she would behave almost like a cornered animal, threatening and throwing rocks or other objects at anyone who attempted to approach her. The principal came to expect that if they were eventually able to restrain Taylor and move her to the office block, any room she entered would be trashed. Taylor had serious learning difficulties and had a lot of trouble making friends. She sometimes made sexual comments at the most inappropriate times and this caused all sorts of issues for her classmates and her teachers.

• • •

It is so difficult to comprehend why students like Rodney, Garry and Taylor would behave in such a disturbing and self-harming way at such a young age. It is equally as challenging to understand why our usual or traditional behaviour management systems and strategies would have so little impact on their behaviours or even sometimes make things worse. We are going to leave these three students for a while — but I ask that you keep them in the back of your mind as you continue to read as we will revisit their cases later in the book.

Chapter Two
Attachment and trauma

Let's talk about attachment

When trying to understand the complex worlds and concerning and perplexing behaviours of young students such as Rodney, Garry and Taylor, we need to consider and combine three theories. ***Child development theory*** explains how a child's body and mind develops as he grows. ***Attachment theory*** examines the impact of early childhood bonding experiences between child and carer and ***trauma theory*** explores the impact of trauma on childhood development. In a nutshell, trauma (particularly abuse and neglect) during infancy and early childhood can have significant impact on a child's early attachment to his caregiver and this can then impact on his future behaviours, his capacity to negotiate future relationships and even his mental health. The reasoning behind this is becoming more apparent through a growing and extremely intriguing body of research. It is very much related to the impact of trauma on the developing physiology (brain and body) of the infant and young child.

Attachment starts in early childhood
Attachment is not something parents do to their children. Rather, it is an unseen but powerful bonding dynamic that evolves with time as children and parents interrelate and respond

to each other within a reciprocal, enduring, physical and emotional affiliation. Attachment provides the foundation for child development; the secure base from which young children learn to explore and relate to their physical, personal and social worlds. When a baby is born, he is predisposed to attach or attune and it does not take long before the infant begins to develop a primary attachment to a preferred caregiver or caregivers (usually parents and most often, the mother). Young children will seek out the company and attention of primary attachment figures when they are in need of sustenance, comfort and reassurance. As children grow, other attachments will develop, but primary attachments during this early phase of life typically remain with the parents or the persons acting in a parenting role.

Instinctual attachment behaviour in the infant is activated by cues or signals from the parent and attachment behaviour in the parent is activated by cues from the baby. Even during the first weeks of life you can observe this intriguing and balanced interaction as parent and child gaze into each other's eyes and respond to each other's cues of distress and delight. You can observe parents doing all sorts of wild and wonderful things with their voices, faces and bodies to encourage and to soothe their babies and you can see how infants react to each of these efforts.

Even more intriguing is what is occurring within the brains of the babies and the parents during these interactions. Imagine mum is holding her infant son on her knee and they are facing each other. Baby scrunches up his little face and cries; maybe as a result of experiencing pain, discomfort or hunger or perhaps from being startled. Almost immediately, you will see mum's face drop; her facial expression and emotional response will quite quickly mirror that of her baby and she will start making soothing sounds and movements to try to minimise her baby's distress. Now, imagine dad is cradling his baby daughter. He has an exaggerated smile on his face, his eyes are bright and he is making silly, musical sounds as he stares brightly into his little girl's eyes.

His daughter stretches her arms and legs and responds with a beautiful, big, open-mouth smile and almost immediately makes a happy, chuckling noise.

If we were able to scan the electrical activity occurring in the brains of these duos during these interactions, we would observe an incredible, patterned response. When the baby boy was expressing his distress, particular neurons (nerve cells) in particular parts of his brain were firing. This neural activity would have had a direct relationship to the emotional and motor activity exhibited by the child while lying on his mother's lap. Almost immediately after this activity occurred, the same type of neurons in the same parts of mum's brain will have fired in response and this would have led to her facial expressions and emotional response almost mirroring that of her baby. Similarly, when the father was expressing his joy to his daughter, specific neurons in particular parts of his brain were lighting up. With little delay, the little girl's brain responded in the same way and quite soon her face, body and verbal utterances match, quite neatly, his joyous manner. Because of the way these neurons work, they have been dubbed, "mirror neurons" and they play an enormously important role in the attachment process as it establishes a reciprocal, regulatory system in which the baby and caregiver influence one another throughout this early development stage.

Becoming safe, secure and emotionally regulated

Eventually, as the infant develops and patterns of caring interactions are repeated again and again, the attachment between parent and child becomes more sophisticated and active. The parent becomes a source of safety and refuge for the young child as he first attempts to explore his world through crawling and then walking, running and play. As this source of security, the parent is trusted by the child to allow for his exploration but is also expected to be available in those moments when he needs reassurance or to be emotionally "topped up".

Consider the behaviours of a toddler who is being introduced by his mother to a playground scenario for the first time. Very likely, the child will want to sit on his mother's knee for a while to observe. Eventually, he might become comfortable enough to start exploring the playground activities and relationships, but only if his mother directly accompanies him. After repeated efforts, he should become courageous enough to explore his environment and interact with others on his own, but you might see him regularly looking over to where his mother is sitting, checking that she is still there, watching and available. When the toddler experiences fear or becomes overstimulated in some other way, he is likely to run back to his mother and jump into her arms until he feels calmed. Then off he will go again to play, explore and relate.

At this age, the parent is the means through which the child's emotions are regulated. Any exposure to stress is repeatedly followed by protection and comfort. Stimulation and soothing occurs again and again in predictable patterns as the child grows and develops. This continues until he becomes more and more competent in self-soothing and regulating his own emotions. Eventually, he will develop a capacity to rely on his internal sense of security and, as a result, will start to establish a sense of emotional resilience.

The impact of trauma

Unfortunately, this journey from healthy, early attachment experiences through to emotional resilience is not available for all children. Consider the infant who cries for attention because his nappy is dirty or because he is hungry. Sometimes the baby is picked up by his mother, who soothes and cares for him. Sometimes, however, he is screamed at and told to shut up. Sometimes, he is just ignored, he goes hungry, he develops painful nappy rash and he is frightened and confused and alone. Sometimes he is even shaken or hit. Now consider the toddler who runs to her father to be calmed and raises her arms to be picked up. Sometimes, she is picked up. Sometimes, she is hit over the head and yelled at to go away. Sometimes, she cannot access her parent because he might be drunk, asleep or absent. Sometimes, she is cuddled and cared for by her father but this is occasionally followed by her being physically or sexually harmed. Sometimes, her father just smothers her in affection while he cries and holds her tightly, because at that moment, her father is distressed and in need of parenting and his daughter is the only one around.

For young children such as these, there is no predictable, repeated response from their caregiver to their communicative efforts. The parent's cues are confusing and the child's cues are often misread. The mirror neuron effect is not working well. Signs of distress from the child can be laughed at and signs of joy can result in parental anger. The parent tends not to become the source of security for the child as they grow. Emotional self-regulation may not develop well and the capacity for successful socialisation and the development of inner resilience may be significantly impaired. In addition, the child must live with the perplexing situation of having the same person representing both the source of their protection and the source of their distress.

These types of early childhood experiences can lead to children becoming either disassociated and withdrawn or becoming hyperaroused, highly anxious and demanding. Both of these states can place maltreated children at further risk. The disassociated (or inhibited) child can become placid and therefore in a situation whereby they can be more easily victimised. The behaviours of the demanding (or disinhibited) child can exacerbate angry and violent responses from the adults in their worlds.

Some of these infants and children are removed from their abusive or neglectful homes and placed in an out-of-home context such as foster care or accommodation programs but many, despite the quality of care and commitment of subsequent caregivers, may prove to be very difficult to manage, even years later. Sadly, another group continues to experience destructive caregiving, abuse and neglect for more of their childhood and sometimes even into their adolescence.

Bowlby and Ainsworth: Two early theorists with important messages

British psychoanalyst John Bowlby formulated the basic tenets of "attachment theory" during his early studies of the interaction between parenting behaviours and child development in the 1940s and 1950s. Bowlby's work was further developed during the 1960s and 1970s by Canadian psychologist, Mary Ainsworth, when she developed a methodology to categorise different types of attachment between child and carer. The work of these two theorists has been instrumental in guiding research into child development and also subsequent studies of the impact that different types of attachment can have throughout the lifespan. In recent years, attachment theory has been used to inform a variety of fields that include individual and family therapy programs, parenting skill development programs and child protection services. Even more recently, this information is gradually getting out to schools to inform how we can better support and educate these students with histories of poor attachment and trauma.

Bowlby suggested that attachment had a number of important functions during the early childhood years and that these also had a significant impact on later life.

1. Of course, the core function of a healthy attachment between caregiver and infant is to meet the **safety and protection needs for a vulnerable infant or young child.** An attuned, loving and protective carer would provide the necessary shelter and sustenance for the young child to survive and thrive and would also do all that they could to protect him from harm. Children with a healthy attachment experience tend to feel confident and secure in relatively safe contexts (such as home and school). However, children with

poor attachment can feel anxious and fearful even in non-threatening environments.
2. Healthy attachment allows the young child to **explore their environment with feelings of safety and security** and this can lead to healthy cognitive and social development as they mature. However, the child with poor attachment can often feel unsafe, unprotected, unsupported and alone and, as a result, their cognitive and social development can be negatively affected.
3. Healthy attachment helps a child **learn basic trust** and this can serve as a basis for all future emotional relationships. Infants learn to expect that their carer will respond to their needs when they cry. Children learn to trust that adults will reassure and calm them when they feel frightened. Unfortunately, children with poor attachment can have significant trouble trusting others and this can impact on relationships throughout their childhood, schooling years and adulthood.
4. Healthy attachment allows the child to initially co-regulate their emotions with the help of their carer and then to eventually build the **capability to self-regulate.** This leads to more effective management of impulses and emotions as they grow. It can help them to develop emotional resilience and **a defence against stress and trauma.** However, those with poor attachment can have difficulty with emotional self-regulation and can very quickly become easily stressed and to become impulsive and/or aggressive when emotionally aroused. It can inhibit the development of resilience and resourcefulness when under duress.
5. Healthy attachment creates the foundation for the **formation of identity and sense of self.** This can include attributes such as self-competence and self-worth and can also lead to a healthy balance between dependence and

autonomy. However, poor attachment can result in children having poor self-worth and a belief that others do not value them. They can become clingy or over-dependant or alternatively, become distant and relationally cold.
6. Healthy attachment can help to **establish a pro-social, moral outlook** in a young person that involves empathy and compassion. However, these attributes are not easily evident in those with poor attachment and they can struggle with understanding the needs, thoughts or actions of others.
7. Healthy attachment helps to generate a **world view that people and life are basically good**, with reasonable exceptions. However, those with poor attachment can believe the worst of most people and of life and it is not unusual for them to exhibit signs of depression, anxiety and/or some form of self-harming behaviours.

So through the early work of Bowlby, and the abundant, subsequent research based on attachment theory, we are better able to understand the importance and impact of the early bond between carer and child. However, it was the work of Mary Ainsworth that led us to being able to identify subcategories of "poor" attachment and ways to remedy them through parenting and other interventions.

Ainsworth developed an experimental procedure known as the **strange situation**. The strange situation involved placing the parent and the child in a room and observing and filming their interactions from behind a two-way mirror. After the child settled and was involved in play, a stressor was introduced by either a stranger entering the room and attempting to interact with the child and/or the parent leaving the room. After a short period of time the stressor was removed or reduced by the stranger leaving and/or the parent returning to the room. The parent and child's responses to being separated, but more importantly, to being reunited, were recorded, analysed and categorised. Ainsworth suggested that these responses and categories may not only reflect the history of the parent–child relationship and the parenting style, but may also predict the child's later psychosocial functioning.

Ainsworth described two broad categories of attachment; *secure* and *insecure*. Within the strange situation experiment, **secure attachment** is displayed when the infant or child uses the parent as a source of security when playing and exploring and then seeks contact with them after separation. The child may be upset when the parent leaves the room but the distress is not excessive. The pair tends to greet one another actively and warmly upon reunion and the child is able to emotionally regulate and soon return to play.

Ainsworth went on to describe three subgroups within the **insecure attachment** category.

1. The **resistant attachment** style (sometimes referred to as ambivalent) may be displayed where the child becomes extremely distressed by the separation, clinging to their parent and often moving to or staying near the door showing visible signs of distress. They may seek contact upon the reunion but tend not to settle emotionally and may even seem to become angry with the parent. They seem to both desire and repel parental contact and support. Within this category, parents may not have been consistently or adequately responsive to their child's needs. They may have exhibited poor timing in response to their child's distress and may exhibit a pattern of obtrusively interrupting their child's play.

2. The **avoidant attachment** style may be illustrated where the child avoids the parent upon reunion or approaches her only indirectly. The infant or child tends to show little or no distress when the parent leaves and actively avoids and ignores the parent upon reunion, often looking down or away, even when in the parent's arms. Historically, this parent

may have also avoided the child or, at least, emotional engagement with the child. They may have been unresponsive to their child's needs and tended to avoid the child's attempts to get close.

At this point, those of you who are parents who are reading this book may be becoming concerned about the damage you might have done to your own children by not responding to them in the most appropriate way, one hundred per cent of the time. My advice to you is to calm down and keep reading! There is abundant evidence now that nature is quite forgiving in most instances and that being a normal and sometimes fallible mum or dad is quite okay.

Research has shown that the bulk of children are securely attached and even moderate levels of attunement with your child's needs will usually result in a secure attachment. Attunement and responsiveness within a primary attachment relationship between carer and child can fluctuate and this is completely normal and expected. It results from the natural variation in the availability, awareness and affect of carers and their children over time. Within normal parameters, both parent and child do quite well and, indeed, children develop a healthy sense of self and a developmentally appropriate capacity for relationships and emotional self-regulation.

It is, of course, always advisable to put effort into your parenting and to repair and rebuild any aspects of your bond with your child after any form of disruption to the relationship. However, do understand that insecure attachment is an outcome of a chronic, consistent and detrimental pattern of non-attunement between parent and child and is certainly not the result of being a "less-than-perfect" parent some of the time.

It is the third and following subcategory of insecure attachment that we will be focusing on for the remainder of this book. This style is representative of parenting relationships typically associated with a high-risk home environment and often child maltreatment. Carers may be psychologically distressed and may be living with unresolved attachment issues from their own childhood and they can appear to be either frightened by and/or be seen as frightening by their children. It is the children in this group that have the greatest risk for later social, behavioural and mental wellbeing concerns because without significant support and intervention, this attachment style can lead to concerning impairment of the child's ability to regulate their emotions and to manage their relationships across their lifespan. This, of course, presents schools with substantial challenges when enrolling students with this type of insecure attachment.

3. The **disorganised attachment** style is evident where there is no predictable or effective pattern of behaviours exhibited by the stressed infant or child to elicit caregiving from their parent. In the strange situation, you might observe a variety of contradictory and quite disturbing behavioural responses. Young children may display a mixture of strong attachment, then anger, followed by avoidance and looking quite dazed. The child may seek closeness and yet avoid it at the same time, through behaviours such as approaching the parent with their head averted or by walking or crawling backwards or sideways. The child may look away from their carer, rather than toward them, when distressed or frightened. Some children have exhibited asymmetrical creeping (moving only one side of the body), mistimed or sudden movements, strange postures or repeated movements such as rocking, hair twisting or ear pulling. Some have even held frozen postures, such as holding their arms raised and immobile for long periods, while others have displayed evidence of extreme fear, flinging their hands over their faces, running away or hiding or crawling into a foetal position.

The neurological and physiological impact of disorganised attachment

But why is this? Why is it that parenting interactions at such an early age can have such a detrimental and often persistent effect on child development and behaviour? For decades, we were only able to study the impact of trauma and attachment on child development by experiments like the strange situation and through direct brain study during autopsy. However, now there is a range of sophisticated brain scanning technologies that has been utilised to significantly progress our understanding in this field, including computerised axial tomography, magnetic resonance imaging and positron emission tomography.

As a result, we now have more evidence than ever before about the effect of trauma and disorganised attachment on the child's brain and subsequent systems in the body. So, to further our understanding, we are now going to explore what I like to refer to as the "science lesson". We are going to look into the actual physiology of the developing child and to examine the impact that attachment and trauma can have on the child's body as it develops.

It is vital that school personnel understand this "science" so that they can comprehend why students from trauma histories behave the way they do at school and they can go on to appreciate why the practices that are recommended later in this book are both appropriate and necessary.

Chapter Three
The science lesson

The nervous system

Very simply, through healthy early attachment experiences gained through caregiving, the young child's **nervous system** develops in a healthy way and becomes a key system for intercellular communication throughout the lifespan. With our cells communicating in a healthy way, our bodies are more likely to be healthy and our behaviours are more likely to be adaptive and constructive.

Basically, the body's nervous system is made up of multiple systems of interconnecting neurons and can be divided into two important subsystems; the **central nervous system** and the **peripheral nervous system**. The central nervous system is formed by the **brain** and the **spinal cord** and is full of interconnected neurons that transmit information between the brain and the rest of body. The peripheral nervous system has two further components.

- The **somatic nervous system** receives sensory information from the environment and sends it to the brain. The brain can then send electrochemical messages to motor neurons throughout the body as its job is to move skeletal muscles. This is easily illustrated by your motor response to touching

something very hot or by moving your hands to cover your ears to block out a loud noise.
- The **autonomic nervous system** comprises of a further two subsystems. The first is the **parasympathetic nervous system,** which manages automatic, routine bodily activities such as circulation and respiration. The second is the **sympathetic nervous system,** which helps our body to prepare for and protect itself from perceived threat.

To better understand the impact of attachment and trauma on child development, it is very important to understand the functions of this latter subsystem; the **sympathetic nervous system**. Once a threat is perceived, this system can cause us to attack, run away or hide; often referred to as the "fight, flight or freeze" response. With the "fight or flight" response, the sympathetic nervous system can slow down digestion and divert blood away from the stomach so as to redirect it to the muscles. It can increase the heart rate, dilate the pupils and cause the hairs on our body and head to stand erect. The adrenal gland increases the release of the hormone adrenaline throughout our system. As a result of all this physiological activity, our bodies become faster and stronger and more able to address any perceived threat by "fighting" or "fleeing". Alternatively, if fight or flight is not an option, our system may help us to "freeze". It can slow heart rate and respiration and cause the body to become very still and hypervigilant. Chemicals such as endorphins are released that help us to stay very still or even to become somewhat numb and less susceptible to pain. When the threat is no longer perceived, our brain releases other chemicals to reverse these effects and this helps us to relax and calm. Our physiology adjusts and we no longer feel the need to fight or run or hide.

The sympathetic nervous system serves a very important function for our self-preservation, but sometimes it does come to the rescue when it is least needed or wanted. We can still feel a surge of anxiety and experience physiological symptoms such as tremors, perspiration, a dry mouth and a racing heart — or perhaps even a freezing response, when we perceive a threat that does not actually exist. As an example, the experience of speaking in public may lead to this response for some people, despite the fact that the audience does not actually present a threat to the speaker's safety or wellbeing. It is vital to remember here that it is the **perception of threat**, rather than the actual existence of threat, that initiates the sympathetic nervous system response.

The human brain

Of course, the brain is central to governing the functions of the entire nervous system. The brain is an incredible and extremely complex organ deserving of the volumes of texts that have been written in an attempt to describe and understand its complexities and functions. However, very simply for the purposes of this book, we are going to divide the human brain into four distinct areas; the brain stem, the cerebellum, the limbic system and the cortex. Each of these areas manages an impressive range of functions and each integrates with the others to govern human development and experience.

The **brain stem** is where the spinal cord merges into the brain. It is the first part of the brain to develop and it is the most developed part when a baby is born. This area manages core regulatory functions that are vital to human survival, including body temperature, heart rate, respiration and blood pressure. As this part of the brain completes most of its development in utero, it is susceptible to harm during pregnancy from circumstances including extreme maternal stress or chemical or substance misuse. If this part of the brain suffers during this early developmental stage, the impact on the physiology of the young child can be significant. It is also this area of the brain that becomes particularly active during the fight, flight, or freeze response described earlier.

The **cerebellum** is situated next to the brain stem at the rear of the head and is the part of the brain that mostly manages bodily movement. It helps us with balance and posture, with control of rhythmic and other movements and to know and manage the position of our body in space. In humans, this part of the brain is not fully developed at birth but continues to mature over the first years of life. This is why human babies take more time than their animal counterparts to learn to control their movements and eventually walk and run. This leaves young children far more dependent on their carers to meet their basic needs due to a lack of mobility. (In contrast, the brains of newly hatched reptiles include a developed brain stem and cerebellum, making these creatures fully able to respond and move according to their safety and survival needs from birth. For this reason, these parts of the brain are often referred to in the literature as the "reptilian brain".)

The next general part of the brain to complete most of its development is the **limbic system.** It is situated in the subcortical or inner parts of the brain, unseen from the outside. The limbic system mostly manages the human experiences of attachment and emotion. It helps us to relate and connect with others. It helps us to process the range of human emotions including joy, fear and anger and assists us to associate a human emotion with a thought or memory. Two important parts of this system are the **amygdala**, which helps us to regulate emotional responses that guide behaviour, and the **hippocampus**, which has an important role in learning and memory. The development of the limbic system is mostly completed by three to four years of age. (Non-human mammals have brains that consist of the brain stem, the cerebellum and the limbic system. The literature refers to this as the "mammalian brain". It is this emotional part of brain that allows particular mammals such as a pet dog to relationally connect with humans and to become distressed by their absence, unlike their reptilian cousins.)

The **cortex** comprises of a number of complex layers forming the exterior of the brain. It also completes much of its development during childhood but remains more malleable according to human experience and learning over time than the other parts of the brain. The cortex is divided into two hemispheres, each with four lobes (frontal, temporal, occipital and parietal) that regulate all sorts of functions that make up what it is to be a human being, including language and managing sensory input and interpretation. The hemispheres are connected by a short bridging area called the **corpus callosum**.

The **prefrontal cortex** (just under the forehead) is only found in humans and regulates the most complex and highly human functions such as higher level and abstract thinking, negotiating, planning and decision-making. The prefrontal cortex is the final part of the brain to complete development with this usually occurring in the mid-to late-20s.

Now that we know some detail about particular parts of the brain, it is important that we consider the concept of "**plasticity**". This term is used to describe the brain's capacity to change and adapt in response to stimulus. In recent decades, studies have provided us with far more information about this potential for change in the brain than we knew in previous times. We now know that different parts of the brain are more or less plastic. The brain stem, for example, is far less malleable than the limbic system, which is far less plastic than the cortex. We also know that overall plasticity reduces with age but that some potential for plasticity remains throughout the lifespan, which is why we can continue to learn. We also know that there are "critical" or "sensitive" periods during which particular parts of the brain are more plastic, and therefore more susceptible to change, than others. Early childhood is a clear example of a sensitive period for development in the limbic system.

It is the rapid development of the brain during early childhood that explains why very young children are so at risk for the lasting effects of trauma. The same plasticity that allows young brains to quickly learn, communicate, relate and feel, also makes them highly susceptible to negative and harmful experiences. This harm can be exacerbated if the source of the trauma is the adult who is their main attachment figure; the one on whom they are dependent for their survival and emotional and relational needs. It is this susceptibility that can lead to at-risk young children having serious and long-term emotional, relational and behavioural outcomes that can prove immensely challenging to those who aim to support or relate to them.

Neurons and synaptic activity

To truly appreciate how normal and abnormal brain development occurs, it is necessary to go a bit deeper and describe neural activity at the cellular level. It is important to understand that all brain development and function is the result of neurons (nerve cells) communicating with each other through an electrochemical language.

Neurons are the basic units that make up the nervous system. Each neuron generally has a set of **dendrites** (branch-like extensions) that receive electrical input from neighbouring neurons. This electrical impulse travels to the **cell body** (which contains the **nucleus and genetic material**) and down through to the end of the **axon** (a long extension) until it reaches small **terminal buttons**. Each terminal button contains tiny sacs called **synaptic vesicles** that contain chemicals referred to as **neurotransmitters**.

There are quite an array of different types of these neurotransmitters, with many having the capacity to influence behaviour, mental health and learning. These chemicals have the amazing ability to transmit information from one neuron to another. When the electrical impulse reaches the terminal buttons, the vesicles open up and release the neurochemicals into a microscopic gap between their original neuron and the dendrites of a neighbouring neuron. This tiny space is called the **synapse**. Some of the chemicals may then bind with receptors (proteins) on the neighbouring dendrites and this can have one of two responses. It can either cause the electrical impulse to continue along to the new cell or it can inhibit the impulse so it does not continue.

This is really a very simplistic description of what occurs during neural activity as the brain of a newborn infant (for example) has over 100 billion neurons, with each having around 2,500 synapses managing the complex chemical interactions of a range of different neurotransmitters. However, it is important to understand the basic process described in the paragraphs above, to grasp the impact of trauma on brain development during early childhood.

The early childhood brain

As explained earlier, the early childhood brain grows and develops faster than at any other stage in their lives and the way that it develops in these early years is critical. All experience is filtered through the child's senses and signals are sent to the brain and this can alter how the child understands and responds to experiences and information. In the first few years of life, the neurons develop vital synaptic connections that influence the child's emotional, social and intellectual make-up. By age 2 or 3, neural development has increased to around 15,000 synapses per neuron.

As the infant or young child interacts with his world, experiences result in patterns of neurological stimuli occurring in the brain. This occurs when neurons repeatedly fire, one after another, in a predictable and repeated sequence. These are referred to as **neural "pathways"**. It is during this time of rapid development that important pathways are established. The more often a pathway is stimulated, the stronger and more resilient it becomes. Areas that lack stimulation, or where stimulation is more erratic, develop weaker synaptic contacts and the pathways degrade. Gradually, a process called **synaptic pruning** occurs, where weaker synaptic contacts are eliminated while stronger connections are kept and reinforced. This is how the plastic nature of the brain is explained at the neural level. It is actually this development and pruning of connections and pathways that allows the brain to change with learning.

Under healthy conditions, pruning can be very beneficial because, as learning occurs, helpful pathways can be strengthened and unhelpful ones can be removed. However, if a developing baby or young child is experiencing the intense stimulus of ongoing trauma, neural activity can be erratic and maladaptive. Consider the situation where the responses of a primary caregiver to a young child are unpredictable; sometimes threatening and abusive, sometimes ignoring and neglecting and sometimes smothering with attention. The adaptive and healthy neural pathways that would occur within a healthy social development would not receive the repeated reinforcement they require to survive in this context. What could otherwise be helpful synaptic connections would be weakened and perhaps pruned away. Conversely, non-helpful connections might be strengthened if the child's young body was repeatedly in a state of high arousal and his neural systems would be consistently battling to regulate his anxiety. It makes complete sense that the brain development of a child living in this type of traumatic social world is going to suffer and if his brain is suffering at this early and critical period of development, it is very likely that there will be emotional and behavioural outcomes throughout out his childhood, adolescence and adulthood.

While we might have considered child **neglect** as less of a concern when compared to child abuse, studies have now shown that it can have a cruel and extremely detrimental impact on brain development. Neglect can involve a failure to meet a child's physical, cognitive, emotional or social needs and each of these domains can have a significant impact on neural development. Malnutrition, for example, can lead to delayed brain development and impaired electrical communication between neurons. The brains of young children who receive little or poor communication from adults, who are not held and cuddled or who are not responded to when they become frightened, or are hurting, hungry or thirsty, tend to lack the stimulation required for healthy neural activity and growth. Indeed, neurological scans from severely neglected children show smaller brains (less mass), high electrical activity in the "survival" parts of the brain (brain stem) and low activity in the cortical areas.

Chapter Four
What does this look like at school?

Calm, healthy students will interact with their school world mostly via the cortex. When experiencing some stress, some brain activity might shift to the subcortical areas in order to heighten their senses and to help them detect and deal with any perceived threat or upset. However, these parts of the brain will have healthy neural connections to the cortex and they will mostly be able to manage the ups and downs of the school day, either independently or with a little help from others.

Fight, flight or freeze!
Students suffering from disorganised attachment and trauma histories tend to present at school with either disinhibited behaviours (hyperarousal) or inhibited behaviours (hypoarousal). Both states result from repeated exposure to chronic stress during early childhood that has led to maladaptive and disorganised neural development. As a result, both states have a very low threshold for stress. Neural pathways have been sensitised to a fear response with little stimulation from the outside world. These children arrive at the school gate with already raised levels of stress hormones in their bloodstreams and far more rapid pulse rates than their non-traumatised peers.

If they become fearful, they will rely more on lower and faster regions of the brain and less and less on the cortex. When experiencing terror, the responses of a child or young person will come from the brain stem, the survival part of the brain. When neural activity in the brain stem is on overload, activity from the frontal cortex is inhibited, severely limiting the capacity to apply logic or to problem-solve to settle the emotion-driven limbic system and therefore calm feelings and behavioural responses. Behavioural responses at this stage are purely reflexive and under little conscious control by the student.

The threat systems inbuilt into the brains of students with disorganised attachment who have lived with trauma, become sensitised to keep them in stares of arousal most of the time. It is therefore difficult for their brains to achieve the calm required for cortical learning. This can then lead to them experiencing learning difficulties, struggling with the curriculum and behaving poorly to avoid academic work and possibly the embarrassment of their lack of academic capacity becoming known to others (particularly to their peers).

At times they can appear fine. However, within certain conditions, it may takes little for them to overreact to environmental triggers that most students would not find threatening at all. Depending on their life experience, they might be overly sensitive to certain facial expressions or loud voices, to sound, a particular smell, touch or physical proximity to others. To most students these same stimuli would be perceived as benign, but for the traumatised student they can trigger fear or terror and an overwhelming stress reaction. When this happens, the fight, flight or freeze response takes over.

Hyperarousal usually results in the **fight or flight** response. Young students might bite or kick or spit. Older students might punch, knock over furniture and yell. Both might run from or storm out of the classroom or school grounds. Both will take a considerable amount of time and careful support to calm. Both might use limited language aside from swearing and short threatening statements.

There is growing research suggesting that this type of disorganised brain activity impacts on children and young people's **oral language capabilities**. Students will often be unable to successfully use language to explain themselves, to settle themselves or to resolve conflict between themselves and others. And of course, interactions with students with poor speech and language skills can quickly deteriorate into hostility and threats when miscommunication occurs and when they overdepend on the words they know and use well, which are usually unsavoury and not received well within a school context.

Hypoarousal usually results in the **freeze** response. These students have historically been unable to fight or run away and so their brain development allows for them to dissociate as a way to cope with their perceived threat. As another survival response, dissociation prepares the body for injury. Blood is shifted away from limbs and the heart rate slows to reduce any blood loss if it occurs. Chemicals (opioids) are released to the brain, reducing the sense of pain, producing calm and a sense of psychological distance from event. Students might curl up into the foetal position and make themselves small. They might sob or cry for help. They might look dazed and be uncommunicative. They might act much younger than their chronological age. A dissociative response is more common in infants and young children and also with females. It is also less likely to be detected at school than the hyperarousal presentation but is equally as concerning and deserving of attention.

Revisiting Rodney, Garry and Taylor

Let's reflect back to our three students from Chapter One. We have looked at how they presented behaviourally at school. Now let's examine their attachment histories to further explain these presentations.

Rodney

Rodney was the young thief. Rodney's mother was married to man with dark features and dark eyes. She had three children and Rodney was the middle child, the result of a much regretted, extramarital relationship. Rodney's fair complexion and blue eyes contrasted significantly to the facial features of his siblings. He was constantly told by his mother that he was a mistake and not wanted. He experienced much verbal and emotional abuse from birth onwards from both his mother and siblings. His physical and emotional needs were also neglected. Rodney's mother often denied him food. She would eat in front of him and would share the food with his siblings but he was not allowed to partake. As Rodney's stealing and hoarding behaviours developed, his mother clasped padlocks on all the cupboards in the home and on the refrigerator. Rodney's siblings were treated far better than he and his stepfather was emotionally disconnected from Rodney from birth.

Garry

Garry was born as the third child to his mother during a time when she was in a very problematic relationship. As he and his two sisters grew, there were further troublesome relationships between his mother and other partners, many of whom lived temporarily in their home and a number of whom were aggressive towards the children and toward their mother. Garry's mother was a past victim of child abuse and was a substance abuser over the years. She was regularly overusing alcohol and prescription medication and was suffering a serious depressive illness. The family lived in very poor circumstances. Garry's mother regularly had extreme outbursts of anger where she hit and screamed at the children and there were times when she would call the schools, the Family Services Department and the Police and tell them she no longer wanted her son or daughters and demanded for them to be taken away. There were also frequent sessions where she would cry and hold her children and tell them how much she loved them. Mum slept for much of the day and, as a result, the children were often either truant or late to school.

Taylor

Taylor had had been living with differing foster families for most of her life as a result of her being seriously and repeatedly sexually assaulted by close family members. She had exhibited extremely difficult behaviours in most foster homes from an early age. As a result, she was regularly moved from home to home when the challenges she presented became too difficult for her carers to manage. Often, when her home placement changed, so did her school. Taylor started creating her own safe space whenever she moved to a new home or commenced at a new school, as this was the only "home" that she felt she could control. Taylor was diagnosed with posttraumatic stress disorder by the age of 9. She often suffered severe nightmares when asleep and concerning flashbacks when awake.

From the surface evidence, it is reasonably easy to see or imagine the harm done by child abuse and neglect as reflected in these three cases. However, neuroscience has made it very clear that it is the inner and unseen damage inflicted by trauma and disorganised attachment — the impact on the developing brains and bodies of very young children — that can have such significant and long-term emotional and behavioural outcomes. Children like Rodney, Garry and Taylor are not your usual "naughty" behaviour management cases and it makes sense that usual behaviour management practices in schools will most likely not work with students such as these.

Unfortunately, without careful support and intervention, the prognosis for young people with disorganised attachment or trauma histories is often poor and their trajectory in life often proves to be problematic. There can be understandable incidences of serious behavioural problems, suspension and expulsion from school, emotional and relationship difficulties, aggressive or self-harming behaviours, substance abuse during adolescence and possible involvement in criminal behaviours. Also, very sadly, these young people are very likely to grow up and parent their own children in the same damaging manner — leading to the intergenerational transmission of disorganised attachment that we are seeing in our populations. Indeed, parents exhibiting damaging behaviours towards their children have often been found to have been unresolved with regards to their own attachment and child trauma histories.

So, neuroscience helps to explain why these students behave in the way they do at school and in their broader lives. However, it also presents us with some very welcome news. There is now abundant evidence that young people are not as "hardwired" as we used to believe. Although the bulk of neural development does occur in early childhood, the incredibly plastic nature of the brain does allow for more "wiring" and "rewiring" later in life. With the right approaches, based firmly on what we now know from neuroscience, there are many things that can be done throughout the school years to enhance the education and life chances of young people living with trauma histories.

Chapter Five

What can we do about this — that works?

In this chapter, we will be exploring approaches that can help the young student's brain to function in more adaptive neurological patterns so that their behaviours at school, at home, towards themselves and towards others can be far more healthy and helpful. First, we will introduce the two key elements of recommended student behaviour support:

1. **Relationships** (strategies to reinforce healthy neurological pathways supporting interpersonal interactions with adults, peers and self)
2. **Emotional self-regulation** (effective calming strategies for the emotionally aroused student, ways to minimise a crisis event and healthy ways to address crisis when it does occur)

After this, we will look into a model for student support that any school can adopt and adapt and finally, we will examine an array of strategies and approaches that are evidence-based and highly recommended.

Relationships (both the problem and the solution)

We now know that the disorganised neural activity of students with trauma histories leads to relational impairment. These students will particularly struggle (and often fail) with relationships in the school setting and this is the bad news. The good news is that all the evidence we now have about the neurobiological workings of the brain has provided solid direction that working on relationships during the school years has huge potential for the adaptive "rewiring" of the brain that is so very needed and so very possible for these young people.

There is also a body of research that has explored the concept of resiliency, which has contributed great learnings for us in this area. This research suggests that not all young people from trauma histories suffer the detrimental effects of disorganised attachment, despite their primary caregivers being the source of the trauma. Those who exhibit resilience in this area tend to have had at least one, supportive, ongoing, constructive relationship with a caring adult throughout their schooling years. If not this, they may have had shorter-term but consecutive relationships of this nature. Merging this information with what we now know of healing aspects of neurobiology, we have solid evidence that working on relationships with these students is vital and this will underpin any success we achieve in other areas, including their academic learning and overall wellbeing.

I will go out on a limb here and state that it is possible that the quality of the teacher–student relationship may be the most important factor for positive adaptation to school. Of course, there should also be helpful relationships with other significant adults within the school, but the class teacher is very important. If the child is no longer experiencing trauma, it has been shown that close, caring and supportive student–teacher relationships can result in enhanced neurological function and improved behavioural and overall wellbeing outcomes for the child suffering disorganised attachment. This relationship may just provide the safety and emotional security under stress that the student so desperately needs and may also allow for healthy neural development. We see the best progress made with these students when we have a capable, caring and informed teacher taking a key role in student support. These teachers tend to remain relationally available to the student, yet they balance this with a carefully defined, professional distance. They do not establish themselves as the best friend, or the parent or the rescuer, but as a wise, strong, kind, resilient and available teacher.

It is important that we realise that many of our behaviour management practices are underpinned by the assumption that students know how to "do relationships". We assume that they can understand and can respond to the concepts of authority, respect, trust, obedience and remorse — when their brains might actually be wired to respond to cruelty, mistrust and survival. Rather, than believing that the adults in the school are basically kind and responsible people aiming to provide an education, they may view them as uncaring and manipulative.

When behaviour management practices are implemented in this context, they are most likely to fail. Without significant work on relationships, rewards will be viewed as manipulation and punishments as cruel. Withdrawal from class, detention, suspension or expulsion will not only reduce any opportunity for relationships, but just might reinforce the maladaptive and negative world views of these students. Whereas your average, "healthy" student would respond to such a consequence in a way to avoid it happening again in the future (that is, to modify their behaviour appropriately), students with disorganised attachment may become more entrenched in their negative ways of dealing with their worlds. In short, what we commonly depend on to manage student behaviour may actually make things worse for these students.

It is understandable that the social dynamics of a busy school present a relationally impaired student with many and regular anxiety-provoking situations throughout the day that can initiate the sympathetic nervous system response and the resultant challenging behaviour. So what we end up seeing is a child or adolescent who refuses to work, who causes problems for their peers, and who is physically and verbally aggressive and very disrespectful. We respond to this by raising our voices, giving and demanding eye contact, requesting reasons and apologies for the behaviour and removing the student from the activity, class or school. We might isolate them from others by placing them in withdrawal rooms or sending them to detention. We might send them home, allocate them to a lower behaviour level in our school-wide system, suspend or even expel them. These types of responses then reinforce their beliefs that they are unwanted, that they will always be rejected and that people are basically cruel and uncaring.

Despite their arrogant persona, students who have experienced abuse can be particularly sensitive to feeling shameful and can respond very badly when these feelings arise. I like to refer to this as a "shame switch". We all have one, but in these young students, these "switches" are extremely sensitive. Shame is different to guilt. Guilt is something you can do something about. You can address guilt by attempting to fix the issue that led to your guilt. However, shame is internal. It can be perceived as part of you and not fixable by changing your behaviour. It can require careful therapy and supportive, caring relationships to address the shame experienced by some young people with very troubling histories, particularly those who have been victims of sexual abuse. However, do not expect to see the outward signs of shame in the faces, voices and behaviours of these students as they can be expert at keeping them hidden.

It is important that we realise early that working on relationships with these students will test the resilience of the adults involved. Attachment-disordered students may put up many barriers to relating, with only the most insistent and committed of teachers being able to break through to them. Once relationships are established, many of these students can experience an overwhelming need to test them. They often believe that they are unlikeable and unloveable and they can become determined to test and retest this hypothesis by sabotaging even the strongest of relationships. They expect you to reject them. This can be very confronting or even insulting to someone who has put so much effort into a relationship with a troubled student and who held the belief that the student valued both the bond and their efforts to maintain it. It is vital that teachers recognise and understand that students' behaviour reflects their relationship history and their maladaptive strategies for coping with stress and relatedness and it is important that they do not take it personally. This is easier said than done, but is an important capacity of the resilient teacher.

With such difficulties with relating well to their regular teachers, it is understandable that these students can have extreme difficulty with relating appropriately to relief or visiting teachers or teachers of specialist classes or with the changing number of subject and support teachers in the secondary school. What we usually see as a result, is extremely challenging behaviour.

These students may also have difficulty with managing peer relationships. Group work, oral presentations, public performances, team sports or games may result in unmanageable anxiety and very confronting behaviours. Often a trauma history can lead to an overwhelming need to be on alert and to control one's environment and, as a result, students may exhibit what may be perceived as selfish and controlling behaviours towards their peers. A lack of ability to read the faces, voices and body language of others can lead to misinterpretation and misunderstandings, fights and disagreements. Relating to peers often involves the automatic management of sensory information, and yet some students from a trauma history may have extreme difficulty with touch, proximity to others, loud noises or maybe even certain smells that evoke difficult memories. Busy playgrounds and student assemblies can be the scene for aggressive outbursts and even simply lining up with their peers can lead to sensory overload for some students. Teachers can be very confused by the perceived overreaction of some of these students to a simple touch on the shoulder or even just to someone standing or sitting close to them.

It is also understandable that a student who cannot "do relationships" will have trouble learning. Accessing the curriculum is very much dependent on the ability to manage one's physical and social environment. A student needs to be able to trust and respect the information giver (teacher), to ignore one's concerns and other stimuli and concentrate on the teaching, to manage peer-based learning experiences, to be able to store and recall information well and to be able to scaffold new information on previous learning. With a chronic inability to relate and to deal with environmental stimuli, students from trauma histories can end up with huge gaps in their learning that arise from the regular physical, emotional or cognitive absence from the learning environment that they experience during their school years.

Emotional self-regulation

In addition to issues with relating, students from trauma histories can emotionally dysregulate regularly and most days will involve some form of behavioural outbursts or tantrums. Schools need to develop both proactive and reactive approaches to enhancing the student's capacity for self-regulation. With the implementation of careful and informed, proactive strategies, students can develop considerable resilience in this area and this can lead to a much reduced frequency of concerning behaviour. However, it is still very likely that, every so often, a significant behavioural outburst will occur and schools need to be ready and able to react in an evidence-based and supportive manner.

During perceived threat and a resultant, significant behaviour event, the student's **endocrine system** can excrete too much of two important hormones. The adrenal glands (just above the kidneys) immediately release **adrenalin**. If the threat is perceived as severe or persists after a couple of minutes, the adrenal glands then release **cortisol**. Once in the brain, cortisol remains much longer than does adrenalin, where it continues to affect brain cells. Usually, a homeostatic mechanism eventually kicks in and the cortisol reduces. However, in the case of the traumatised student, a chronic oversecretion of these stress hormones can occur, which can adversely affect brain function and can certainly make emotional self-regulation very difficult to achieve. Furthermore, too much cortisol can damage the hippocampus, which is central to learning and memory.

If school personnel intervene with a disciplinary response after a student behavioural outburst, but before allowing time for the cortisol to dissipate, they can be putting themselves, the student and others at risk from a further outburst. It is recommended that at least 30 minutes of low stimulus activity (perhaps colouring in) is provided for younger students and up to an hour or even more for adolescents, before any questioning or behavioural interventions are attempted.

Even then, this must be done in an informed and caring manner that takes into consideration the student's individual circumstances. School personnel must also consider the impact on the hippocampus and the possibility that the student may not have accurate recall of the details of the behavioural event. This lack of communication and recall can easily be misread as their avoiding discussion or refusing to relay information or, at the worst, blatantly lying, when it may actually be due to confusion and an impaired access to memories.

Six-element model for student support

Case management of students with disorganised attachment and challenging behaviour tends to be more successful if the following six aspects of support planning are addressed well. Alternatively, if these aspects are ignored, things can become very difficult at school.

1. Establish a strong support team.
2. Inform your team about neuroscience and current research.

3. Get to know and understand your student.
4. Engage the support of the broader school community.
5. Look after the people who are looking after the student.
6. Develop a support plan addressing:
    - Relationships
    - Emotional Regulation (including both proactive measures and a crisis response)

1. It is vital that you **establish a strong support team.** It should never be expected that the teacher alone is responsible for the support of such a complex student. The team should be led by a responsible and informed case manager who is not the class teacher. Members of the team need to be chosen carefully. They need be reasonably resilient and collegial and willing to learn and adapt their practice. They need to be willing to share the load and to meet regularly to review and advance support planning. Members may also include district or regional education support specialists or representatives from other government or non-government child or adolescent support agencies. Your principal or school leader needs to be involved or, at the very least, informed as it is she who needs to approve any decision-making. If there is no team approach to support, we tend to see an extremely detrimental impact on the wellbeing of the teacher or the student, or both. There tend to be clashes in beliefs from colleagues about what should or should not be done, particular personnel become overwhelmed and constructive supports are not put in place.
2. You need to **inform your team about evidence-based research** in this field. Source and share readings, websites and other resources to build the knowledge and understanding of your team regarding *Type 2 Trauma and Disorganised Attachment*. Your local youth mental health or child protec-

tion services would be a good source for this type of information. If your team's work is not founded on this information, you might find that you will fall back on traditional management practices that will not work or you will be arguing with your colleagues about ways to manage the case.

3. **The team must grow in their understanding of the student.** You need go through files, speak with previous teachers and schools and any previous or current support agencies or specialists involved with the student. You need to discover what the key issues are for this student and what has been proven to work or not work in the past. Key people need to spend time with and getting to know the student. If this is neglected, the team might adopt practices that are not congruent with the individual needs and peculiarities of their particular student and this could cause more harm than good.

4. **The support of the broader school community needs to be sought and engaged.** I cannot understate the importance of whole-staff support, as it is possibly the most important element for the success or failure of support planning. The bulk of behavioural outbursts that lead to crisis outcomes tend to arise from interactions between the student and one or more adults in the school who are unaware, unskilled or unsupported in responding well to the student's emotional dysregulation. This can happen in the playground, in specialist lessons or in the classroom when a new or uninformed teacher takes over the class. You also find that without whole-staff support, the team will need to persistently argue with their colleagues to support their planning and actions. This is unfair on the team and certainly not supportive of the student.

Engaging whole-school support does not come without its challenges as you need to balance the need for this support with the student's right to privacy and confidentiality. Schools should always respect that there are aspects of such a student's life history and experience that are not for public knowledge, particularly in the case of sexual abuse. However, there are ethically appropriate ways to achieve this level of confidentiality. You could try giving your support team a particular title. The title is not as important as is the whole staff understanding that when a team with this title is in place, there are very significant and valid reasons why planning around a particular student needs to be supported without enquiry. You could also engage the authority of the principal. School leaders can speak to their personnel about their expectations for whole-staff support for the recommendations from the team and their expectation that no further questions are asked.

You may think of other ways to achieve this level of confidentiality, but it is important that these strategies are also supported by whole-school training in the knowledge and understanding of the impact of trauma and disorganised attachment. The bulk of school personnel do not need the depth of understanding that would be expected of the team, but basic knowledge is very necessary. As examples, this can be achieved through short training sessions during staff meetings, engaging guest speakers or through required readings.

Once this level of support is achieved, the team and the broader staff could work together to develop supportive classroom, playground and specialist lesson procedures. In secondary school, it would be important to engage each teacher who has this student in their class. A procedure for informing and supporting any relief teachers should be developed and ideally, you should try to minimise the number of relief teachers that would be working with the student, (as much as possible) to those who are informed and capable in this area of student support.

5. It is also vital that you **look after the people who are looking after the student**! Teachers and other staff members who are committed to working regularly, even daily with this young student need to be supported. Without support, people can burn out or become isolated, overwhelmed or depressed. They can even be physically hurt. Ultimately, under these conditions, student support will fail. Collegial support is extremely important. Respite and opportunities for key personnel to discuss, debrief and recharge should be organised. Regular case meetings should be provided. It is acknowledged that often the last thing a busy teacher feels they need is another meeting, but I find that teachers usually really appreciate this type of support when they are managing a student facing these types of challenges. These teachers need to be heard, they want fresh ideas and they need to know they are supported and appreciated.

6. You will need to **develop a support plan.** It does not necessarily matter what format is used, but it is vital that this plan focuses on support processes and is not merely a list of behaviours expected of the student and consequences for behavioural breaches. The plan needs to draw from appropriate practices and strategies that are grounded in solid research about the neurological and physiological needs of the student. If this is neglected, different staff members may be doing things in different ways and important elements may be neglected. The overall goal of the plan should be the student's development of more adaptive representations of (and behaviours towards) themselves and others. The planning needs to be individualised according to the needs of the particular student and it is vital that it focuses on the two key areas of **relationships** and **emotional self-regulation**. It must also include planning to teach and reinforce **self-calming strategies**, as well as **crisis management and response**. Depending on the student, this planning may take

precedence over planning for the student's academic achievement as the capacity to learn is very much dependent on the capacity to relate and emotionally regulate.

A list of recommended strategies and approaches

The strategies and approaches listed in this section are some examples that can address either relationships or emotional self-regulation or both, depending on how they are used. It is important to acknowledge up front, that every student and each school context is deserving of an individualised approach and that there are no "one size fits all" strategies. Remember to choose strategies that may work on the specific relational, emotional and behavioural issues of your particular student with a trauma background.

Mentoring

Identify and train one adult in the school to act as a significant other and mentor for the student. This person should be available for regular contact during which the focus is on developing skills in relating and managing the stress response. This person should be called upon to assist during and after any crisis involving the school with their input focusing on emotional recovery from the situation and the repairing of damaged relationships. This person should not be the class teacher but should be willing and able to support the class teacher.

Check in and check out

This strategy is particularly helpful for students who arrive at school already emotionally aroused or who need calming after breaks or help with transitions. The student checks in with the mentor before school begins and receives reassurance and support to meet their current needs. In the morning, the mentor can check if the student has had breakfast, if he has the requisites needed for class work and if he needs some cool-down time before entering class. Check out can happen at the end of the day with a reassuring message that the student will be welcomed back the following day. With new students or those having particular difficulties, check in can happen after any lunch or other break causing concern. This strategy will require some planning as the mentor will need time (and perhaps resources such as pencils or access to the canteen) to support the student and the student needs to be provided with a process that allows them to be late to class at times (such as a signature-card system).

Pick your battles

Remember that these students have unusually elevated anxiety levels most of the time and it takes little for that to escalate further and quite a while for cortisol levels to reduce. It is important that serious behaviours are addressed (carefully), but it may not be worth engaging in power struggles with these students over lesser behaviours. A simple example would be when a student responds poorly to being asked to pick up a paper lying on the ground. Any ensuing power struggle is likely to lead to a quick and severe escalation in behaviour that could end up with significant consequences for the staff member (perhaps injury) or the student (perhaps expulsion) — all of which started over a piece of paper. This is a good example of why all personnel working at the school need to be informed about this student's support needs. This will prevent unhelpful adult–student interactions and will also prevent other staff members assuming and worrying that the class teacher or the support team are being "too soft" on the student. This concern about being "too soft" is one that is based on a number of beliefs, including that a firm stand will be good for the student and also that the behaviours of other students might escalate if one student "gets away with" poor behaviour. When all those working at the school have a basic understanding of the neurological and physiological circumstances associated with the student stress response, behavioural crises can be averted and collegial support can be enhanced.

Using codes and symbols

You can develop a teacher–student communication system that may help to alleviate concerning student behaviours and reinforce positive relationships. Such a system is particularly helpful for students who find it difficult to explain themselves in public or when emotionally aroused. Signs can include hand gestures (thumbs up or down), sounds (tap on the desk) or written symbols or words on cards. They can be initiated by the teacher or the student, depending on the reason for the sign or symbol. They will look different according to the developmental stage of the student, the relationship between student and teacher and the reason for the sign or symbol. An adolescent will have a very different system with his physical education teacher compared to one that is used by a young preschooler and his class teacher. A student may use a different sign to access teacher assistance to that used to let the teacher know he is becoming upset or angry. A teacher might use a sign to provide some type of emotional reassurance to the student if she suspects a student is becoming anxious. It may also prove helpful to allow the student to come up with a sign or symbol that is meaningful to them or to keep the meaning of the sign or symbol private between the teacher and student so as to minimise any peer response. It is important that you use this strategy sparingly and do not confuse the student by using multiple signs or symbols. Just reserve this strategy to enhance the important parts of your support planning for the student.

This strategy will be shaped by the individual circumstances of the student, but some ideas are listed below.

- Use a card with the word "SOON" written on it as a strategy for managing students who are continually trying to access teacher attention in inappropriate ways. Teach the student that the unspoken message when they are given the card is that the teacher is aware that he feels he needs attention and that she will attend to him soon. If you do use this strategy, you do need to keep your promise and get back to the student in a timely manner. As the student becomes more used to waiting and trusting that you will be there, the time between the card-giving and the attention can grow.

- A student can have green, yellow and red cards in their desk and can display one at a time on top of his desk representing how he is feeling (for example: green = okay, yellow = uneasy, red = angry). This can help the student articulate and manage their feelings and can also help the teacher to respond early to prevent any behavioural outburst.
- A student might have a small object or toy in their pocket that is an agreed symbol between themselves and the teacher that (for example) the teacher cares about them. They can hold or fiddle with this object or toy to help them emotionally regulate.
- A student might have an agreed hand gesture that he can show his teacher to let her know that he needs to leave the room for a short time to calm himself.

An example of a helpful use of gesture was used with a Year 1 girl who had suffered terrible trauma in her short years and who presented with highly disruptive and challenging behaviour in the classroom. After some trial and error, a secret code was developed by the teacher whereby she would take the child's hand and give it three gentle squeezes. The agreed and unspoken message behind this gesture was, "I really, really, really like you". When the teacher used this simple strategy, the student was more likely to settle, become compliant and engage with class activity. If a brain scan could be done at that moment, you would be likely to see the electrical activity in the brain stem and the limbic and cortical areas of the brain start to adapt and regulate. By the way, a lovely endnote to this story occurred a few years later. The student had left the school after her first year due to a number of changes in her foster placement but was re-enrolled again in Year 4. On her first day back at the school, her original teacher was on playground duty and noticed a young girl running across the school yard in in her direction. The girl almost ran into the teacher, grabbed her hand and (you guessed it), squeezed it three times. A terrific example of a simple and, in this case, memorable strategy that worked on both relationships and emotional regulation for this young student.

Scaling

Scaling is a strategy to assist emotional regulation that can be used in numerous ways and can be adapted according the needs and circumstances of the student. Initially, some time needs to be spent with the student helping them to understand the different stages of their emotional arousal. You might use words like "calm–worried–scared–terrified" to represent a scale for an anxious student. Words like "happy–sad–upset–angry–furious" might represent a scale for a student having difficulty with anger and aggression. Alternatively, some students might prefer to come up with their own descriptors that are more meaningful for them.

Once there is a shared understanding of the meaning of the words on the scale, you can engage the student in a gradual process of tracking and recording his emotional patterns throughout the school day. A secondary student might simply circle the words on the scale at different times of the day or might prefer to use a numerical system to keep their scaling activity more private. You might use graphics or colours for a younger student or one who is struggling with literacy.

The teacher or the mentor can spend a short period of time reviewing the patterns in the scaling records each session or each day, depending on need. You can talk about classes or times that prove more difficult for the student and ways to help. You can co-develop strategies to help them calm or to remove themselves proactively from a stressful environment or situation. You can celebrate with them when their efforts show a reduction in concerning patterns in their scaling records.

Scaling can be used according to the needs of the student. Some use it to help students communicate their emotional state non-verbally to a supportive adult. For example, a student might have a set of small cards on their desk with symbols or colours on them that represent stages of emotional arousal. They can place the one most representative of their current state on the top of the pile so that the teacher can know when they need help. Others use it as a tool to directly assist a student with their efforts to emotionally regulate. For example, a series of chairs, each painted a different colour according to a scale, can be placed outside a classroom or near a play area. The student (or students) can choose to sit in the chair representing their emotional state and move to adjacent chairs as they calm themselves (with or without the help of adults). While sitting in the chairs, they can practise their agreed self-regulation skills. This could be breathing techniques, drawing or colouring or repeating calming cognitive scripts (thoughts). These techniques need to be designed by or acceptable to the student and never imposed upon them.

Look for the gold in every child

No matter how challenging the behaviour of any student there is always something wonderful about them, if you take the time to get to know them well. Finding this "gold" in the child can be very therapeutic for relationships. You might discover that although some of these students have extreme difficulty relating to people, they might be terrific with animals. You can capitalise on this to teach them about relationships. You might find some have a capacity for art or music or construction. You might find some are kind to small children or are protective of their siblings. Look for the gold and often, when you discover it, you will find there is further gold to be found.

Boundaries, rules and consequences

Students with disorganised attachment can experience erratic brain activity, erratic physiological responses and erratic behavioural control. Just as with any student, they need help to develop self-control though the establishment of behavioural boundaries, rules and expectations. They also need to experience consequences for their behavioural breaches. However, we need to acknowledge that their capacity to adhere to rules and to learn from consequences may be significantly impaired and they will need time to develop the required skills and understandings. They need to be allowed (even expected) to fail and to be encouraged to try again. Punishments such as social withdrawal and suspension rarely work with these students as we are denying them the relational medicine that they so desperately need to be cured. What they really need is to experience unconditional concern and sincere forgiveness and help to repair relationships and address any harm that they may have caused.

A better way to manage detentions

Rather than resorting to excluding practices (such as detention) as punishments or consequences for poor behaviour, try to create opportunities for relating and teaching. This might mean that, although the student misses out on play time during lunch, they still spend that time in an activity with an informed adult who acts in a caring manner. The adult can help the student reflect on their behaviour and develop an understanding of the concerns surrounding that behaviour and even develop a plan for how they could repair some of the damage caused by the behaviour (natural consequences). It is important that schools recognise that this is not a "soft" option. Rather, it is a process by which you are applying neurobiological understandings that are far more likely to result in enhanced positive behaviours and decreased negative behaviours than if excluding consequences are used to isolate the student.

Relational rewards

Just as relational consequences are more likely to be helpful, so too are relational rewards. Rather than relying on symbolic or token rewards (stickers, toys, time on the computer), it is helpful to plan relational rewards for these students. Examples might include time to play a board game with a teacher or time playing ball with a peer. Although these students do not "do" relationships very well, they are certainly relationship thirsty. Thus, it is likely that a relational reward would have a greater capacity for success and again provides opportunity for that adaptive neural rewiring we are all striving to achieve.

Movement and rhythm activities

Approximately half of the cells in a human brain are in the cerebellum or movement centre of the brain, which is understandable because much of who we are and what we do is expressed through bodily movement. The human cerebellum can take much longer to mature than in some non-human counterparts, which is evident when you compare how long a child takes to learn to walk and run, compared to a foal or a puppy (as examples). This leaves children very dependent on the care of their parents for an extended period. In healthy, early childhood attachment contexts parents spend considerable time rocking their young babies and encouraging and teaching them to meet their motor milestones (sitting, crawling, walking, etc.). Infants are not born with a sense of rhythm but rather this is stimulated by the early rocking activity that helps to regulate neural development in the cerebellum. Unfortunately, many children from trauma (particularly neglect) histories with disorganised attachment can exhibit difficulties with rhythm and at times appear quite clumsy. Research has also identified important neural connections between the cerebellum and the frontal cortex, which implies that there is an important neurological relationship between movement and learning that can be hampered through early childhood trauma.

Schools can help with the neurological development and rewiring in this area by including rhythmic and motor development activities in the daily program, particularly in early childhood or primary school contexts. A few examples of activities that have proven helpful include music, dancing, drumming, ball bouncing and other games, and playing on swings and trampolines. An imaginative teacher could more than likely think of many more activities that could prove advantageous for these children and could easily incorporate this type of activity into whole-class events. The benefits are not only in motor development but also evident in learning and motivation.

Predictability

Traumatised children and young people can experience change as disconcerting. They can become overly hypervigilant in a new or changed environment or circumstance as their brains tend to be wired to respond quickly to perceived or potential threat. It is important that the school day for these students is as predictable as possible so that the stress of the unfamiliar is minimised. To help address these concerns, teachers can use strategies such as visual cues and timetables, consistency and repetition, and timed warnings before the end of activities or lessons. It is also important to prepare students for managing change prior to it occurring. For example, it is valuable to work on strategies for coping with days when the usual teacher is absent and a relief teacher is taking the class, or to practise coping with transitions between activities or classes.

Helping students relate to other students

For relationally impaired students, it is advisable that you work on relationships with key adults first and then engage those adults to help the student work on peer relationships. In the arena of peer interaction, social rules are implicit and picked up mostly by observation and trial and error, rather than by direct instruction. These rules can change readily and are not necessarily viewed as fair by all parties. Violating these social rules can be far less tolerated than when the student is interacting in the world of informed and supportive adults. Students will need help to understand and negotiate these rules and to become resilient when they make a mistake or when things do not go their way. Explicit **social modelling** and **coaching** is recommended as body language and social cues may be unintelligible to some of these students.

An adult at the school can model helpful social behaviour for the student, by using her own behaviours in a social situation and then afterwards narrating for the student what she did and why she did it. This could occur during an early childhood craft activity, in a primary school playground or during a soccer game with adolescents. The adult can then coach the student as he attempts to interact with peers in a similar situation that was previously modelled for him. Over time, success with other students should make the student less socially awkward and reactive. However, he will need lots of opportunity to repeatedly practise and be reassured when he fails and encouraged to try again. The adult supporting the student needs to remember that this repetitive modelling and coaching activity is aiming to develop adaptive neural pathways in the young student's brain that will serve them well for years into their adulthood.

It is important for teachers to remember that some of these students will have much difficulty with understanding the thoughts and feelings experienced by others and this can present as a lack of empathy. Rather than judging this as a personality deficit, it is more helpful to recognise it as a neurological issue that can be addressed with kind and consistent teaching about relationships and, in some more serious cases, some therapeutic interventions by trained counsellors.

Social behaviours and physical contact

Young students who come from a trauma history (particularly sexual abuse) may experience difficulty with modulating appropriate physical contact with adults and peers. They may hug or jump onto the laps of adults at the school (even those they do not know well). They may stand too close or rub up against others. They may not seem to know when to establish or break eye contact. They may exhibit what should be private behaviours in public spaces, which can range from wiping their noses to touching their genitals.

Ironically, children with attachment problems will often initiate physical contact (hugs, holding hands, crawling into laps) with strangers. Adults can misinterpret this as affectionate behaviour but it is important we realise it is a maladaptive response that can place the student (particularly young children) at further risk. How adults handle this physical contact is very important. We should not refuse to hug a child or to lecture them about "appropriate behaviour." However, we can gently teach them about ways to interact appropriately and safely with adults and other students who they do not know well and it is important to do this in a way that does not make the child feel bad or guilty.

• • •

The strategies and approaches listed throughout this chapter are but examples of activities and processes. Teachers and other educators are resourceful and creative professionals who should be encouraged to develop further strategies that might suit the relational and emotional regulation needs of particular students. Remember that these strategies may need to be used again and again, as challenging the way the pathways in the brain work takes time, consistency and repetition! It is very important that we continue to remind ourselves that it is far more effective for schools to adopt evidence-based practices informed by neuroscience than if they depend solely on traditional or generalist behaviour management approaches and strategies.

Chapter Six
Crisis management

Preparing for and managing a behaviour crisis

When planning for student support it is vital that crisis management is considered. It is equally important that the support team and the school in general expect crises with students suffering disorganised attachment, because it is very likely to happen. When it does, the physiology of this student will dictate their emotions and behaviours and schools need to have a plan to address the immediate safety and wellbeing needs of the student, their peers and staff. However, it is equally as important that the school has an agreed plan for what needs to be done after the crisis is over. Crisis management for these students needs to consider both **proactive, reactive and reparative** measures.

Proactive measures should include careful observation and data collection to help staff recognise signs of anxiety in the student or any triggers to that anxiety. Steps then need to be taken to minimise any opportunity for those triggers to occur. A **"safe space"** needs to be organised for the student to retreat to when they are feeling emotionally aroused, and they need ample opportunity to practise retreating to this space during "low arousal" times, to help make this retreat more of an automatic response. It is also helpful to help the student develop and practise anxiety reduction techniques that he might be comfortable using. Depending on the student, this might include breathing techniques, going for a run, bouncing a ball or colouring in. It is also beneficial to engage the help of the student's mentor during early signs of arousal.

Reactive measures need also to be planned. Any documentation regarding crisis responses needs to be read and understood by anyone who will be working with the student. The document should articulate what is likely to be happening within the student physiologically and also what types of behaviour might be expected. It should also articulate the responsibilities of the particular adults who should respond to the crisis. Again, it is useful to engage the help of the student's mentor at this time.

During severe dysregulation the student's brain stem will be doing most of the work and will be focusing on perceived risk and survival. The frontal cortex will not be working as it should, so questioning the student or expecting them to engage in a logical discussion will not be helpful at this time. The hippocampus will be affected, so memory and recall will be impaired. The amygdala will be working on overload, so emotional responses will be virtually under no conscious control. Stress hormones will be surging through the student's circulatory system and the electrochemical activity occurring in the brain will be highly disorganised, so physical responses may be maladaptive and disturbing and verbal responses may be limited to silence, repetitive swearing and cursing or illogical or incoherent outbursts. Those in fight mode may become aggressive and destructive. Those in flight mode may try anything they can to escape. Those in freeze mode may emotionally and psychologically dissociate. Some curl up in a foetal position or hide behind or under furniture or objects. Some present with behaviours from a much earlier developmental stage, such as hugging a toy or sucking a thumb.

At early signs of dysregulation the student should be caringly encouraged to go to their safe space and then given ample time to calm. If they prove to be highly dysregulated, this calming process might take considerable time and the fight, fight, freeze response might ensue until then. In some instances, the student may not make it to the safe space. Staff can expect bad language and physical outbursts and it is important that other students are removed to a safe environment, away from the dysregulated student.

Any physical restraint of the student should be reserved as only a last resort and only for the student's own or other's safety. Damage to property is always unfortunate but should not be the guiding consideration for physical restraint, as restraint can actually make the calming response longer and more difficult. If restraint becomes necessary, it should be done in a calm and reassuring manner by personnel trained in appropriate techniques. All schools should have a people trained in this type of restraint. For very serious cases involving dangerous behaviours, the police might need to be called in to assist.

After the initial crisis is over and the student has started to calm, it is important that the student is left alone (with watchful eyes nearby) or that only those with established rapport with the student engage at this time. No-one should touch the student unless they are absolutely sure that this is going to be helpful and that it is at the invitation of the student. The focus for this time is physiological repair. The student's body will need time to regulate the severely disorganised brain activity and the cocktail of hormones that have just been raging through his system. It may require long periods of silence. The student might cry. Some might dissociate or act developmentally younger. Some students can actually fall asleep. Do not interfere with this process or you could risk reigniting the stress response. Once the student has recovered, it is advisable for them to go home, after a reassuring message from key support workers in the school that they will welcomed back once they feel better. The school then needs to provide ample opportunity for staff debriefing, if requested and wanted, and to start planning for what comes next.

The **reparative measures** to be implemented after the crisis has subsided form the part of the support plan that can be the most troubling and controversial in school communities. Neuropsychology would tell us that the most important response to such a crisis event in a child or young person is inclusive teaching and rebuilding and repair of relationships. It would suggest that punitive or excluding consequences could further exacerbate the relational and emotional concerns for the student. It would also suggest that the crisis should be viewed as an opportunity for learning, rather than an opportunity for punishment.

However, most school policies would articulate that this level of verbal and physical aggression requires serious punitive consequences and this would often include suspension or expulsion. Schools would also be dealing with the concerned parents of students who witnessed and were frightened by the event and the expectation that something be done about the student's behaviour. This presents schools with a serious dilemma that requires a whole-school response that should be carefully articulated, both in the individual student's crisis management plan and in the school's behaviour management policy.

Example of crisis management plan

The following is a template that can be used or adapted to allow for student crisis management planning. Schools can replace the words in parentheses with the details regarding the specific student and the agreed planning. Schools can choose to introduce the plan with an explanation, if deemed appropriate. This same introductory explanation can be documented in the school behaviour management policy.

Crisis Management Plan

Student Name:
Class/Year Level:
Date:

At times, schools enrol students who have lived through very difficult or traumatic life circumstances and, as a result, present with very challenging behaviour at school. These students may need significant help with managing relationships within the school setting. They may also need help with their emotional self-regulation as they may have a very strong fight/flight or freeze response when they feel anxious or threatened. With this type of support, crisis events can be minimised. However, one or more crisis events still may occur during the school year. During crisis, the emotional and physiological responses of these students can be beyond their control and the planned and calm responses of key adults from this school will be required to manage the event both during and after it occurs.

[Note: Research has shown that during and after a crisis event the best emotional, relational and behavioural outcomes can occur for a student if this event is viewed as a learning opportunity, rather than an event that needs a disciplinary response].

It is understandable that staff, students or community members who are present during the crisis, or who hear of the event after the crisis, may be concerned. Please note that all reasonable efforts will be taken to hear and address these concerns, but at no time will confidential information about the student who has experienced the crisis be shared with others without appropriate and informed consent.

Describe how [student] might look and sound during crisis (examples provided below)

- repeated, loud swearing
- makes unfounded accusations towards adults (e.g., accuses them of hurting or hating [him/her])
- pacing back and forth
- avoids eye contact
- knocks over furniture and attempts to damage or throw objects
- red face
- tears in eyes
- has difficulty responding to questions or engaging in conversation.

Proactive measures to minimise the event of a crisis

- Response team identified and aware of roles
  [Provide details here]
- Agreed communication strategy in place to access the response team, carers and external support personnel
  [Provide details here]

- Key mentor relationship in place
  [Provide details here]
- Safe space established for [student]
  [Provide details here}
- [Student] taught during low arousal times how to access and use the safe space
  [Provide details here]
- Self-regulation strategies taught to [student]
  [Provide details here]
- Important phone contacts established and known to key school officers/personnel (e.g. carer/s, police, doctor, therapist, other)
  [Provide details here]

Reactive measures in the event of a crisis
- Implement communication strategy
  - List who is to contact whom and when
  - List the responsibilities of each person when contacted
- Mentor or other trusted adult stays with [student] and attempts to assist [student] to [safe space]
- If [student] presents as too dysregulated to move, move all other students to a supervised and safe space
- Mentor or trusted adult remains within proximity of the student, maintaining a distance so as not to appear threatening to the student. Use quiet, calming, and reassuring statements and periods of silence as required, gradually assisting the student to emotionally regulate
- Mentor or trusted adult reminds [student] that this is what [he/she] has practised and that they will stay with [him/her] and help [him/her] until [he/she] feels better
- Carefully, move objects away from [student] if needed and if does not upset [student]
- Give abundant time for calming. Remember cortisol levels will still be on the rise even after [student] appears to have calmed
- After [student] has calmed, other adults ensure there are no onlookers when [student] is moved to the administration block
- [Agreed calming activity or activities] provided for the student as needed
- Engage the support of carers and other support personnel outlined in the communication strategy

Crisis Management | 75

In some cases, physical restraint may be necessary if [student] is unable to regulate or if [he/she] is unable to be contained in a safe space and others are at risk of harm.

- Trained team assists mentor to restrain [student] using agreed processes and to reassure [student] using calming statements.
[Provide further details here]

If all attempts to calm [student] and to keep [him/her] and others safe prove unsuccessful, implement the following.

- Phone Police/other agreed agency for support.
[Provide contact details here]
- Student to be removed from school site, accompanied by carers and external support personnel.

Reparative work to be done after the crisis.

- Provide opportunity for staff debriefing if needed and requested
- [Student] to stay away from school for [an agreed number of] day/s
- [Mentor] to contact/meet [student] during this time and help [him/her] process the event and to prepare [him/her] for [his/her] return to school
- Prepare [student]'s classmates for [his/her] return to school
[Provide details here]
- Mentor to assist the student to re-engage on the morning they return to school ("fresh start" approach)
[Provide details here]
- Provide time and resources for the class teacher to spend time with the student, focusing on rebuilding and repairing relationships
[Provide details here]

Helping teachers to understand and manage their own reactions and emotions during and after crisis

The importance of your remaining calm (or at the very least pretending to) during interactions with an attachment-disordered student, cannot be understated. This is particularly important for times when a student becomes dysregulated. You will be the means through which the student will eventually co-regulate, similar to how a toddler needs a parent to help them calm down from a severe tantrum. You need to keep a quiet and calm tone of voice and as much as possible, a caring (and not frightened or shocked) look on your face. It helps to remember what the student has been through in their lives to get them to this difficult place and to acknowledge the physiological surges that they are experiencing. Keep talking to a minimum, but do keep reminding the student that you are there to help when they are ready. If you find yourself frightened by the student or unable to maintain calm during a difficult interaction, it is preferable that you remove yourself and allow someone else to take over.

No matter how well adults supporting a child or adolescent during one of these high-level incidents manage such scenes, most will find it to be upsetting. It can be quite disconcerting to see the harmful and aggressive actions and hear the awful language from the student. After the event, when there is time to reflect, it is completely normal to feel upset and shaken. Educators tell of having difficulty sleeping the night after such an event.

Schools need to provide the time and place for any educator who has been through such an event to be able to debrief with someone of their choice. It is helpful if there is a trained counsellor on staff who has the professional skills for allowing the person to tell their story with minimal interruption and without necessarily advising but to encourage and allow for the healing process to begin. Teachers might need some time away from their teaching responsibilities to allow for their feelings to subside. Any adult should be reminded to take time to relax and to connect with family or friends in the wake of an event such as this.

We often find that adults who have an understanding of attachment theory and the impact of trauma on students tend to fare better. They do not tend to question whether it was something they did (or did not do) that led to the event. Rather they acknowledge that these outbursts are very likely for a child of trauma, even in the most supportive of environments. They also seem to be more resilient when it comes to reconnecting well with the student and rebuilding their relationship because they know the importance of this in the overall growth and development of the child or young person.

Considerations for school policy

It is advisable for schools to do three things to minimise concerns regarding crisis events.

- First, the school's behaviour management policy needs to articulate how students with trauma histories will be supported and how the school will respond to any significant behaviours. Perhaps attaching a blank template for a crisis management plan could be helpful.
- Second, the principal or school leader needs to take a firm stance regarding the school's approach to supporting these particular students and needs to outline her expectation for her staff accordingly.
- Finally, this approach to support and crisis management needs to be clearly explained and taught to all school personnel so that that there is whole-of-school support for this approach and that there are no divisive discussions or opinions. It is often very difficult to successfully implement this approach to student support as a minority or as a lone teacher or principal. Whole-staff support is vital and this will initially require some professional growth in understanding the neuroscience underpinning trauma.

Suspension and expulsion

In an ideal world, we would never want to use excluding consequences for relationally impaired students. It is actually the opposite of what they need. However, the behaviours exhibited by these students can, at times, be so complex and severe that it is not unusual for schools to resort to suspension and sometimes expulsion.

John's case is one that illustrates this point.

John's father was verbally and physically abusive towards his wife and child and John's mother died when he was three years of age. John grew up in a remote, country area. His father travelled to access work and John was very often left at home alone. As he grew, John's behaviours become more and more aggressive and disturbing. He often truanted from school and had significant learning difficulties. At 10 years of age, John's father decided he no longer wanted to deal with John's behaviour. He drove him to his maternal aunt's residence (many hours of travel from his own residence) and left him there. His aunt had been trying, unsuccessfully, to gain custody of John since her sister's death so, although now in her late 50s, was happy for John to move in with her.

John was enrolled at a local school and immediately his behaviours caused concern. For the first few months, he regularly ran from class or from school. He swore and was exhibiting physically intimidating behaviours towards both adults and children at the school. After a time, with some very supportive work by his teacher and others at the school, John seemed to settle. However, at home, John was beating his aunt and she was regularly presenting at the school with significant bruising and tears in her eyes, asking for help.

One of his aunt's strategies to control John was to bribe him with gifts. Being a child of neglect, John loved the gifts (and his aunt loved giving them) but they did little to help him control his behaviours. John became very attached to any new gift he was given. He would keep it with him constantly, would refuse to go to school, go to bed late or wake up very early so he could play with, or even just hold, the gift. To him, these items represented relationships. His aunt was the first to give lovely gifts and they helped him feel, what he thought was, love.

At one time, John's aunt promised to him that, if his behaviour improved, he would be given a skateboard. Within days, John had the skateboard, despite no real change in behaviour. He woke up before sunrise one day, hopped on his skateboard and headed to his school. He had a terrific time skating around the empty grounds until the school principal arrived. As such behaviour on school grounds was not allowed, John was told to come to the principal and relinquish the skateboard to him. The next couple of hours involved a variety of staff members trying to chase and apprehend John, which proved very disruptive to the entire school. Eventually, John's skateboard was taken from him. He immediately became seriously dysregulated and began to swear, intimidate with aggressive gestures and eventually throw a barrage of stones and rocks at any staff member or student who came near him. A number of people received minor injuries as a result and the police were called. Eventually, John escaped and went home. The afternoon involved police visits to the home and some significant time with a child psychologist.

The next day, John awoke feeling better and his memory of the day before was hazy and somewhat disjointed. He dressed himself, ate breakfast and went to school. Rather than going to class, as he fully expected would happen, John was kept in the principal's office to be questioned about his behaviours from the day before and to be told of his suspension.

From a purely attachment/trauma view of this situation, a suspension was the last thing that John needed and, indeed, this did lead to more serious behaviours being exhibited towards his aunt and the local community. However, from a school's perspective, it is extremely difficult to avoid giving a significant consequence for such significant behaviour. The principal would be dealing with upset students and staff members and a range of expectations from parents, the community and colleagues to manage the situation appropriately and according to school policy. There would be health and safety concerns and the reputation of the school to consider. These considerations would put the leader of the school in a very difficult place indeed, particularly if they are aware of, and concerned about, the tragic circumstances of the young student's life.

So, in reality, we know that schools are complex communities driven by a multitude of dynamics and pressures and we know that these students do end up suspended or expelled at times. However, despite these disciplinary measures being deemed unavoidable at times, there are ways to "do them better".

If a decision is made to suspend a student, the first consideration is whether or not this could be a more supportive, in-school suspension. The in-school suspension can require that the student does not work from his usual classroom or classrooms but rather from a space away from the other students. However, similar to how this book recommends that a detention is managed, the in-school suspension should involve the management and input of outwardly caring and supportive adults. The student should be expected to complete (or attempt to complete) a work program that is appropriate for his learning needs with regular opportunities to speak with an adult, take a break, eat, drink, and so on The adult (perhaps the student's mentor) should spend time helping the student revisit the behaviours and circumstances that led to the suspension and to analyse why they occurred and ways to avoid this in the future. The in-school suspension should not be viewed as disciplinary and harsh, but rather as a consequence to manage the harm previously done by the student and an opportunity for personal growth in the student in order to minimise the chance of those behaviours occurring again.

Understandably, an in-school suspension is resource-intensive and some schools may not be in the position to be able to offer this option for students. In these cases, a school might decide to implement an external suspension. However, it is important to remember that the longer the student is disconnected from the relationships at the school, the more challenging it could become to reinstate his trust and willingness to engage with people at the school (adults and peers). Therefore, it is recommended to keep suspensions as short as possible or, if this is not an option, to ensure regular contact with the student throughout the suspension. Of course, it is important to check on the student's wellbeing during suspension, particularly if he is living in a problematic home environment. It is equally as important to provide times and places for the student to meet with his mentor or another trusted adult. This adult should provide activities to be achieved during these times with the aim of repairing and rebuilding relationships, discussing and addressing the behaviours of concern and preparing for re-entry to school.

After the suspension is completed, a **"fresh start"** approach should be provided when the student returns to school. This tends to be far more successful than what I refer to as the **"prove yourself"** approach, whereby someone in authority at the school outlines to the student a list of behavioural expectations that they are to meet if they are approved to return. In the bulk of cases, schools do this because of the belief that "drawing a line in the sand" will lead to the student becoming somewhat intimidated into compliance and this does tend to work with many students who do not have a trauma history or disorganised attachment. However, for these students the "prove yourself" approach tends to create even further anxiety and emotional dysregulation which, of course, can lead to further troubling behaviours. We tend to see students already extremely on edge and highly vigilant even before they arrive at school on the day they return from suspension, knowing that they are expected to attend the re-entry meeting. Even if a supportive adult spends time with the student preparing him to cope with his potential reactions to these meetings, outcomes tend to remain poor in many instances.

Students are often expected to meet in the principal's or deputy principal's office; a room that can feel intimidating even at the most benign of times. [Interestingly, parents of students who attend meetings in these rooms are often amazed at the unease that they feel the rooms can evoke in themselves as they reflect on their childhood memories of school.] Unfortunately, for the attachment disordered student, this unease is magnified to worrying levels. The room can be associated with discipline, authority, fear and ultimately, harm. Sometimes, students are seated opposite an imposing desk with the principal on the other side. Sometimes they are seated in a chair and surrounded by adults. Despite the often non-threatening intentions of the adults in the room, the student can feel cornered and at risk. The student's innate mistrust of adults will most likely initiate a fight or flight response that may be dictated by a physiological response they will be unable to control. They will be unable to respond appropriately to the questions being asked of them and will most likely end up swearing, becoming aggressive or running. Of course, this type of response can lead to another suspension.

For these students, this approach to re-entry after suspension is not recommended. Rather, a fresh start approach has more potential for re-engaging the student with the relationships within school, while minimising emotional dysregulation on their return. Any discussion regarding the behaviours that led to the suspension, or behavioural expectations after returning to school, should have occurred when the student was met during the suspension. This is not the business of the first day back.

The first experience a student returning from suspension should encounter, is the opportunity to meet with their mentor (or trusted adult) in a space that they deem as safe and reassuring. The mentor's job is to welcome the student back to school and to gauge their capacity to return to class in an emotionally regulated and constructive manner. If the student needs time to calm, this is given. If he needs to eat or drink, this is provided. The mentor might need to accompany the student into the class or perhaps just to the door (to minimise any embarrassment). The mentor should also check in with the student throughout the day to monitor their status. Everyone at the school should realise that the first day back will be an uneasy one for the student and expectations should be adjusted accordingly. Again, this can contradict our usual thinking regarding behaviour management whereby we would normally refer to behavioural boundaries and high expectations.

If a school enrols a student after expulsion from another school, it is proposed that an approach is used that is similar to that described for helping a student return to school after a suspension. It is important the school is welcoming and that staff members focus on building relationships and minimising the stress response in the student. A "fresh start" approach rather than a "prove yourself" approach is recommended. Schools should avoid any confronting "entry" meetings that involve discussion of the student's previous behaviours and so forth. The student's physiology will already be on high alert and may be exacerbated by such procedures and reinforce the student's misbelief that they will be unwanted and mistreated. Any interactions with the student on that first day should be driven by the knowledge of the student's neurobiological concerns and needs, rather than their behavioural history.

Ideally, prior to that first day, it is recommended that the school be as prepared as possible to receive this new enrolment. Having a support team ready who are informed about attachment and trauma is always recommended. This team should aim to gather important information about the student from documents and people who have previously worked with the student, both from other schools and other support agencies. They should also have spent some quality time with the student's carers. The team should try to have a basic support plan in place that is informed by attachment and trauma theories and which can modify as the school grows in the knowledge of the student after they have attended for a time. The teacher(s) with whom the student will be working, needs to be informed and prepared.

These recommendations frame an ideal approach but, of course, there are many instances when a student is expelled or has to move from a school for another reason and enrols at a new school with little or no prior notice. This does put staff at the school in a challenging position. If at all possible, the school should delay the student's first day until information is gathered and a team approach prepared. If this is not possible, the school needs to work on assumptions gathered from the enrolment interview with the carer and phone contact from the student's previous school and do the best they can until support processes can be put in place.

Moving a student to a new school

If at all possible, it is valuable to invest time in preparing a student with a trauma history, prior to them commencing at a new school. The aim of any preparatory activity is to lessen anxiety levels on the first few days at the new school. This can be helpful when a very young child starts at school or it could involve a student who is changing schools for a variety of reasons, including expulsion. Children in foster care with significant behaviour disorders can experience a number of changes in home (and therefore school) placements throughout their schooling, due to the challenges they present in the home. Careful preparation for their transition to a new school is an important investment that is deserving of time and resources.

Carers, school personnel and workers from child support agencies can collaborate to do this preparatory work. It could involve a couple of initial drives past the school property followed by a number of short, pleasant visits. It might involve school personnel visiting the student at home. It could involve providing the student with a booklet of photographs of key areas and people from the school that can be discussed and explained. The overall goal is to have the student in a calm and supported place by the time that they start day one.

Chapter Seven
Compliance, adolescence and working with parents

Recognise difficulties with compliance for what they are

Students with disorganised attachment may have much difficulty with compliance in a school setting and often a teacher insisting on compliance will end up in an ugly power battle. Part of this difficulty may directly relate to the student's view of adults as being uncaring and manipulative and their view of themselves as unlovable. Part of it may be due to the student's difficulty with complying with adult requests while emotionally dysregulated. Part of it may be that compliance to abusive adults in their childhood might be associated with significant harm. Whatever the reason, they will most likely need help to develop the skills underpinning compliance.

We need to acknowledge that these students may not have an innate tendency to please adults, so when working on relationships with them it is important to have that initial positive impact on some of their misbeliefs and trust issues. We then need to help them communicate to us what compliance looks like and feels like for them. Students might explain that they feel teachers are trying to control them or hurt them or embarrass them. They might feel they are being tricked into getting angry so that the teacher can "kick them out of the classroom". We then need to help them experience some of the positive feelings and outcomes associated with compliance that come so easily for students with secure attachment and are so elusive for those from a trauma history. They need repeated exposure to things such as people wanting to be with them more often when they are compliant, teachers responding kindly and happily when they are compliant, accessing meaningful rewards when they are compliant, feeling proud of their own efforts when they have been compliant. These are not the usual experiences of students with disorganised attachment and we need to help them to gain these helpful experiences and any associated healthy social and emotional outcomes.

Physiological and social concerns in adolescence

Traumatised children and young people can lack the capacity to regulate their own physiology. For example, they may struggle to manage anxiety, put themselves to sleep or regulate their appetites. As they grow older this can become even more difficult and they are likely to start to self-harm or self-medicate in an attempt to obtain some relief and to establish some control over their own bodily functions.

Self-harm can be difficult to understand, but it can be common in traumatised (particularly adolescent) students and school personnel need to be aware of this. The reasons for self-injury can differ between students. Some self-harm because they become addicted to the endorphin release that accompanies traumatic stress and will cause trauma to themselves to obtain that endorphin release. Another group may internalise the aggression of their abuser and then become the victims of their own aggression. Others have developed a profound self-hatred and act this out on their bodies. Some suffer from deep depression and their self-harm is closely associated with a wish to end their pain, which, when severe, can develop into suicidal thoughts. Still others self-harm to overcome the numb and alienated feelings that come from dissociation, where the self-inflicted pain is an attempt to feel something rather than nothing. Some wish for the physical pain or the shock of the sight of blood to overcome their internal pain.

Drugs, alcohol, inhalants and other substances can be used by children and young people living with trauma. Some may also become addicted to high-stimulus activities such as computer games, dance or sexual activity, or engage in high-risk physical behaviours in an attempt to regain a "high" feeling. Some young people find criminal activities highly stimulating and attractive. Unfortunately, without significant support and intervention, time in youth detention or even an adult prison system is not out of the question for some of these young people, as research has shown significant inmate numbers represent people living with unresolved childhood trauma and disorganised attachment.

Students from trauma backgrounds who put themselves at risk in these ways need significant therapeutic and clinical support and it is important that school personnel do not assume that they are engaging in this behaviour to be trendy or because they are copying other students. It is also important that this behaviour is not interpreted as purely attention-seeking, although these students are certainly in need of (and deserving of) attention. It is more often the case that this is a serious and maladaptive coping strategy requiring the collaborative intervention of caring and informed adults. There is a lot more that could be said about these specific behaviours. However, as it is more the responsibility of health and mental health systems than schools, I will not elaborate any further in this book, aside from reinforcing that students living under these circumstances certainly need to be referred for help.

A note on working with parents

Sometimes, it is clear that a student has a trauma history and suffers disorganised attachment and this is often when the child or young person is already in the child protection system. However, sometimes these students are still living with their biological parents and schools are in the difficult position of suspecting that these concerns exist without any actual proof.

There are two extremely important reasons that school personnel do not suggest to parents or carers that they feel their child has disorganised attachment or attachment disorder. First, educators do not have the professional skill or qualifications to diagnose such a concern or conditions and could very easily mistake poor student behaviour for disorder. If disorder is suspected, it is advised that the concerns are shared initially with the school counsellor or psychologist, with a request for follow-up with the family and potential referral for professional help outside of the school if deemed appropriate. Second, whether the child is rightly or wrongly a victim of disorganised attachment, it can be hugely insulting and hurtful to a parent or carer to have this suggested, as the implication is that it is their fault and that you may be suspecting them of abuse or neglect. So, if attachment concerns are suspected, you can still adopt the practices recommended in this book, but do leave the discussion of concerns to professionals qualified in this area.

Sometimes, we can become aware that the parent of a student we know or suspect is suffering disorganised attachment exhibits similar relational and behavioural traits to that of their child. Some may present as argumentative and distrustful and may complain readily. They could present quite regularly at the classroom before or after school to complain about the class or the teacher's behaviours and the negative impact they believe this is having on their child. They might choose to take their complaints to the principal of the school, sometimes on a regular basis. These interactions can become quite aggressive and, at this level, this can become quite a stressful part of the principal's job that is very difficult to address or solve. It can be extremely difficult to satisfy the concerns of such a parent, for when one problem is addressed they can become upset about another. They can elevate their complaints to education departments or politicians or the media, sometimes repeatedly. In very difficult cases, the physical and emotional wellbeing of teachers and principals in this situation can become compromised when having to deal with the repeated confronting visits and phone conversations from such parents and the ensuing reporting and paperwork requirements.

There is not a singular or simple strategy for alleviating a situation like this. The behaviour of these parents can be just as complex and confronting as working with an aggressive student, and can have just as traumatic an impact on school personnel. The bulk of the emotional energy of educators is usually invested in self-defence and it becomes quite difficult for them to develop empathy for such parents. However, from what we know of the intergenerational transmission of disorganised attachment, it is likely that these parents have unresolved trauma histories of their own. It is likely that a number of decades previously they would have been living as children with the complexities that their own children our now facing. It is possible that they have some very concerning memories of their own schooling experience that have left them feeling angry and distrustful of educators and the schooling system.

In almost all cases, these parents truly do desperately love and care about the wellbeing of their children. They are quite sincerely concerned that people in schools are doing harm and that it is their job to prevent this from impacting on their children, perhaps in the way that similar behaviours previously impacted on them. When educators recognise this, they can interpret the parents' concerning behaviours through a different set of lenses. They tend to be able to empathise more easily with the parents' situation and may find themselves with more emotional energy to deal with the situation in a way that does not tear into their own wellbeing.

Schools also need to be aware that, for biological or foster carers, living with an attachment-disordered child or adolescent can be very difficult indeed. In these circumstances, schools need to be understanding and compassionate and need to acknowledge the importance of working together. Problems in the home context will impact on the school and issues at school will impact on the home. Unfortunately, in cases of foster care, difficulties at school and repeated discipline, suspension or expulsion can lead to the inability of a carer to maintain a home placement, which often means a move to a new placement and perhaps another school. This all contributes to ongoing disruptions in attachments experienced during these young and vulnerable lives. It is vital that schools work collaboratively with carers and other professionals involved in the care of students to minimise such disruption, if at all possible.

A final word ...

If we approach the behavioural challenges presented by students who are living with trauma histories and disorganised attachment in a traditional, disciplinary or punitive manner — because we believe that they have the capacity to choose between right and wrong and that they are deliberately choosing what is wrong and defying us — we may be predetermining a very problematic life trajectory.

We need to acknowledge that these young people are experiencing disorganised neural activity and that their brains and bodies are dealing with abnormal amounts and types of neurochemicals and stress hormones during many hours of most days. We need to recognise that these students are relationally impaired and may have serious communication deficits where they have extreme difficulty interpreting social information, faces and voices.

We need to remember that they might be overly sensitive to sensory information (maybe noise, movement, touch, or proximity to others). We need to be aware that they can present as hypervigilant, aggressive or perhaps dissociative. We also need to consider that some of them may have further mental health complications as a result of the trauma they have endured.

We also need to acknowledge that each case is different and is deserving of an individualised approach to support and crisis management. We should certainly not treat them just like we would any other misbehaving, (yet emotionally healthy) young person who would have a far greater capacity to respond well to generalist behaviour management approaches. Indeed, if we do, it is very likely we will be unsuccessful and the behaviours will persist and worsen, the disciplinary measures will become more and more excluding and the intensive needs of these students will not be addressed.

It is vital that schools grow in the understanding of trauma and attachment-related issues and research-supported behaviour management approaches. We need to re-examine those of our own beliefs that just might be presenting us with barriers to helpful change in our practice. We need to refer to valid information backed by research in neuroscience. We need to focus on how to assist these students during their schooling years with human relationships and with emotional regulation. We need to view them as distressed and not merely deliberately defiant!

Bibliography

Berridge, D., Dance, C., Beecham, J., & Field, S. (2008). *Educating difficult adolescents: Effective education for children in public care or with emotional and behavioural difficulties.* London: Jessica Kingsley.

Bombèr, L.M. (2007). *Inside i'm hurting: Practical strategies for supporting children with attachment difficulties in schools.* UK: Worth.

Bombèr, L.M. (2011). *What about me? Inclusive strategies to support pupils with attachment difficulties make it through the school day.* UK: Worth.

Brandell, J.R., & Ringel, S. (2007). *Attachment and dynamic practice: An integrative guide for social workers & other clinicians.* New York: Columbia University Press.

Casaneuva, C., Cross, T.P., Ringeisen, H., & Christ, S.L. (2011). Prevalence, trajectories, and risk factors for depression among caregivers of young children involved in child maltreatment investigations. *Journal of Emotional and Behavioral Disorders, 19*(2), 98–116.

Coch, D., Fischer, K.W., & Dawson, G. (Eds). (2007). *Human behaviour, learning and the developing brain: Atypical development.* New York: Guilford Press.

Coch, D., Fischer, K.W., & Dawson, G. (Eds). (2007). *Human behaviour, learning and the developing brain: Typical development.* New York: Guilford Press.

Cozolino, L. (2006). *The neuroscience of human relationships: Attachment and the developing social brain.* New York, Norton.

Doidge, N. 2008. *The brain that changes itself: Stories of personal triumph from the frontiers of brain science.* New Zealand: Scribe.

Durrant, M. (1995). *Creative strategies for school problems: Solutions for psychologists and teachers.* New York: Norton.

Grossmann, K.E., Grossmann, K., & Waters, E. (Eds). (2005). *Attachment from infancy to adulthood: The major longitudinal studies.* New York: Guildford Press.

Gyamfi, P., Lichtenstein, C., Fluke, J., Xu, Y., Lee, S., & Fisher, S. (2012). The relationship between child welfare involvement and mental health outcomes of young children and their caregivers receiving services in system of care communities. *Journal of Emotional and Behavioral Disorders, 20*(4), 211–225.

James, B. (1994). *Handbook for treatment of attachment-trauma problems in children.* New York: Free Press.

Kraly, F.S. (2009). *The unwell brain: Understanding the psychobiology of mental health.* New York: Norton.

LeDoux, J. (2002). *Synaptic self: How our brains become who we are.* USA: Penguin.

Levy, T.M., & Orlans, M. (2008). *Attachment, trauma and healing: Understanding and treating attachment disorder in children and families.* Washington: Child Welfare League of America.

McCrae, J.S. (2009). Emotional and behavioral problems reported in child welfare over 3 years. *Journal of Emotional and Behavioral Disorders, 17*(1), 17–28.

Newton, R.P. (2008). *The attachment connection: Parenting a secure and confident child using the science of attachment theory.* California: New Harbinger.

Pearce, C. (2009). *A short introduction to attachment and attachment disorder.* London: Jessica Kingsley.

Perry, A. (Ed.). (2009). *Teenagers and attachment: Helping adolescents engage with life and learning.* London: Worth.

Perry, B., & Szalavitz, M. (2007). *The boy who was raised as a dog: And other stories from a child psychiatrist's notebook.* USA: Basic Books.

Ringeisen, H., Casaneuva, C., Cross, T.P., & Urato, M.U. (2009). Mental health and special education services at school entry for children who were involved with the child welfare system as infants. *Journal of Emotional and Behavioral Disorders, 17*(3), 177–192.

Seigel, D.J. (2007). *The mindful brain: Reflection and attunement in the cultivation of well-being.* New York: Mind Your Brain, Inc.

Simmel, C. (2007). Risk and protective factors contributing to the longitudinal psychosocial well-being of adopted foster children. *Journal of Emotional and Behavioral Disorders*, *15*(4), 237–249.

Snow, P., & Powell, M., (2012). Youth (in)justice: Oral language competence in early life and risk for engagement in antisocial behaviour in adolescence. *Trends & Issues in Crime and Criminal Justice*, *435*, 1–6.

Snow, P., & Powell, M. (2011). Oral language competence in incarcerated young offenders: Links with offending severity. *International Journal of Speech-Language Pathology*, *13*(6), 480–489.

Snow, P., & Sanger, D. (2010). Restorative Justice conferencing and the youth offender: Exploring the role of oral language competence. *International Journal of Language & Communication Disorders*, *46*(3), 324–333.

Snow, P.C. (2009). Child maltreatment, mental health and oral language competence: Inviting speech-language pathology to the prevention table. *International Journal of Speech-Language Pathology*, *11*(2), 95–103.

Snow, P.C., & Powell, M.B. (2008). Oral language competence, social skills and high-risk boys: What are juvenile offenders trying to tell us? *Children & Society*, *22*, 16–28.

Solomon, J., & George, C. (Eds). (1999). *Attachment disorganisation*. New York. Guilford Press.

Szalavitz, M., & Perry, B. (2010). *Born to love: Why empathy is essential and endangered*. New York: Harper Collins.

Tabone, J.K., Guterman, N. B., Litrownik, A.J., Dubowitz, H., Isbell, P., English, D.J., Runyan, D.K., & Thompson, R. (2011). Developmental trajectories of behavior problems among children who have experienced maltreatment. *Journal of Emotional and Behavioral Disorders*, *19*(4), 204–216.

Taylor, C. (2010). *A practical guide to caring for children and teenagers with attachment difficulties*. London: Jessica Kingsley.

Walrath, C.M., Ybarra, M.L. Sheehan, A.K., Holden, E.W., & Burns, B.J. (2006). Impact of maltreatment on children served in community mental health programs. *Journal of Emotional and Behavioral Disorders*, *14*(3), 143–156.

Ziegler, D. (2005). *Achieving success with impossible children: How to win the battle of the wills.* Arizona: Acacia.

Zeigler, D. (2001). *Neurological reparative therapy: A roadmap to healing, resiliency and well-being.* Jasper: Jasper Mountain.

Ziegler, D. *Optimum learning environments for traumatized children: How abused children learn best in school.* Retrieved from http://www.jaspermountain.org

CPSIA information can be obtained
at www.ICGtesting.com
Printed in the USA
LVHW081453051118
596005LV00015B/587/P